Move From Surviving to Thriving:

The Positive Psychology Workbook for Challenging Times

First Edition

Bruce W. Smith, Ph.D.

Dear Reader,

This workbook is freely offered to anyone who wants to use it to create a life of greater joy, happiness, meaning, and fulfillment in spite of the challenges we often face.

You have my permission to use anything in this workbook as long as you use it for increasing human happiness and well-being and make it as freely available as you can.

In addition to this printed copy, you can also download as many free PDF copies of the workbook as you like at the following link:

https://drive.google.com/drive/folders/1eVPov4kbw-2WcYHU51Nbv8wi-aCC3y72?usp=sharing

Also, please note that downloading a PDF copy might make it easier for you to watch the videos associated with this workbook. While the links are provided in this workbook, you would need to type the link in whereas if you also download the PDF copy you should be able to just click on the links to get to the videos.

Please feel free to email us at cappnmusa@gmail.com if you have any questions or if the above link is not working.

Warmly,

Bruce W. Smith

Kindle Direct Publishing
Seattle, WA, U.S.A.
ISBN: 9798571856447

Table of Contents

Preface

This workbook is a labor of love and free offering to all who might benefit from it. It is based on my gratitude for years of being able to teach positive psychology and especially to the students and teaching assistants who have taught me so much. It is my attempt with the help of the Center for Applied Positive Psychology in Albuquerque, New Mexico to offer as many people as possible the best of what positive psychology, and broader psychology and science, have to offer to each one of us. Positive psychology is the science of happiness and what makes life worth living and it is bringing the power of modern science to enable all of us make the most of our lives and live them to the fullest.

I first taught positive psychology at the University of New Mexico in 2005 and it quickly became the thing I enjoy doing more than anything else! Since that first class of 30 students, the class has continued to grow to include two face-to-face classes of 200 students every year and another 100-200 students in an online course developed in 2018. The course has been voted the best class at our university more than once and, most important, I have seen how much of a difference it can make in the lives of students and in my own life. Since 2016, my research lab has collected data on how students do during the class and has consistently found that students have significant increases in happiness, well-being, and resilience and decreases in anxiety, depression, and stress.

In the past few years, several community leaders and I joined together to form the Center for Applied Positive Psychology (CAPP) whose mission it is to share the benefits of positive psychology with as many people in as many communities as possible. During the summer of 2020, in response to the uncertainty and stress caused by the COVID-19 pandemic; the people at CAPP and I decided to create a four week "positive psychology challenge" that took the best of what we know about positive psychology to make it available to others. This challenge, as captured in this workbook, includes what those in CAPP and I have found to be most beneficial in our teaching, research, consulting, and personal experience.

Because the initial response to our online challenge was so positive, we decided to make its benefits as broadly available as possible by creating a workbook to enable anyone who wanted to do the challenge whenever they wanted at their own pace. The positive psychology challenge in this workbook includes 24 chapters with lessons that represent the best of positive psychology, the videos that we created to help communicate the lessons, other TED talks and videos that have been highly rated by hundreds of students; questions to help you reflect, learn, and grow; and the activities and exercises that more than anything else can enable you to bring positive psychology to life. Positive psychology is not a spectator sport, but a participatory sport that we can all take part in and it's only when we do that we will really see what it has to offer.

Finally, here comes the best news of all. Positive psychology is not just about surviving, it is about thriving even during the most challenging and stressful times of our lives. Rather than avoiding or denying the bad things that come our way, positive psychology can enable us to face them, prevail, and use them as opportunities for learning and growth. It is for each and every day of our lives – even when we are going through a hard time or trying to deal with loss, failure, or rejection. In fact, you might even say that positive psychology is especially for these times because it enables us to be at our best in all circumstances and make the most of our lives whatever we are going through. More than anything else, the positive psychology that you can come to experience through this workbook will enable you to bring out the best in yourself so that you can live your life to the fullest.

So welcome aboard! You are beginning a wonderful journey on what has to be one of life's greatest adventures. All we ask is that you be open to what you can learn and, most important, try it out for yourself and see what happens!

Bruce W. Smith, Ph.D.
December 7, 2020

Acknowledgements

I began the Preface by saying how grateful I was for the years of being able to teach positive psychology and for all of the students and teaching assistants who have taught me so much. Now is the time to acknowledge my gratitude for those who have contributed and helped most with the development of this workbook.

First, I am grateful to John Freisinger who took the initiative during the summer of 2020 to invite me to work with him and our group in developing a "positive psychology challenge." Despite the fact that we were meeting on Zoom in the throes of a global pandemic, his entrepreneurial spirit was a catalyst that got me and the others at the Center for Applied Positive Psychology (CAPP) going. Soon after, I started writing the lessons and creating videos for them and John put it all together into an online platform that enabled us to pilot the challenge together.

Second, I am grateful to Tanya Kallan, who I have had the great fortune of having as both a student and later as a teaching assistant for my positive psychology classes. Tanya loved the idea of putting our initial challenge into a workbook and volunteered to do what has been the great majority of the work in formatting and putting it together. Moreover, she has done this during a global pandemic and her first semester of graduate school! As anyone who meets her can readily see, she is a shining light who naturally embodies the best of positive psychology. She is contagious with hope, humor, and good cheer and without her this workbook would not have been possible!

Third, John, Tanya, and I are grateful to CAPP, whose mission is to share the wealth of positive psychology as broadly as possible with both individuals and communities. CAPP consists of a rich and diverse group of community leaders in positive psychology including Paul Smith, a co-founder and leader of CAPP, who taught positive psychology to hundreds of employees at Sandia National Laboratories in New Mexico for many years. In addition, Drs. Steve Poland, Swasti Vohra, and Clara Farah are psychologists who have taught and/or are teaching positive psychology in various forms and settings. We are also grateful to Kelly Ward and Joe Dennis who have a wealth of experience bringing positive psychological approaches to work settings that have benefitted countless employees and their families and friends. Finally, there are many others associated with CAPP who have provided support, feedback, and encouragement including Alvin Phan, Matthew Higgins, Mary Lemmond, Nancy Fitzgerald, and Marcia Mikulak.

Fourth, we are all grateful for our students and those we have been able to get to know and work with for giving us the opportunity to learn together about what can really make us happy and our lives worth living. There is no better way to learn positive psychology than seeing it in the lives of other people and there is probably nothing that does more to inspire and bring us hope. We have seen first generation college students who against all odds graduated from college and went on to become doctors, lawyers, teachers, and counselors.

We have seen people confronted by stress, illness, and trauma who have been able to learn, grow, and benefit from the challenging times they experienced and give something back to the world. We have seen how people of all ages, occupations, countries, and cultures can benefit from what they learn and use it to move their lives to new and unexpected higher levels of joy and happiness. We are grateful to all of these for what they have taught and shown to us and for how it will enable this workbook to come to life for you.

Finally, we are most grateful to you for taking the time to read this and make this challenge a part of your life. We hope that you will come to experience the joy and gratitude that we have in learning about and sharing the wealth of the growing discoveries in positive psychology. We wish you all the best in making the most of your lives and living them to the fullest. Thanks for joining us on the journey!

Bruce W. Smith, Ph.D.

How to Use this Workbook

We are so happy you are taking the opportunity to utilize this workbook to help you overcome obstacles and achieve your best life! As you work through the chapters, you will develop a set of tools which use the science and power of positive psychology to your advantage to empower you to thrive – even in the midst of life's challenges.

Before you get started, we want to give you some suggestions about how to use this workbook to best fit with your life and schedule.

As Bruce said in the Preface, this workbook grew out of the positive psychology challenge that we developed with the help of John Freisinger and the Center for Applied Positive Psychology (CAPP). This workbook is something that you can use for yourself, use as part of a group, or lead others in using. The lessons are presented in four parts that build upon each other: (1) Basic Training for Your Best Life, (2) Bringing Out Your Best, (3) Bringing Out the Best Around You, and (4) Creating the Best Possible Future (Part 4).

Since you can move through the topics at whatever pace works best for you and your schedule, you have several options in completing this workbook. You may decide to do the whole workbook in four weeks as a jump start for a new year (or anytime you want to quickly dive in or do a refresher). Or you may want to take it more slowly and complete one, two, or three chapters each week. A slower pace could be a great way to fully savor each topic and dive deeper into each concept. Doing two chapters each week would take three months to complete the workbook. You might find this to be a great way to build new habits. Another idea would be to establish a weekly Cultivating My Best Life Day, for example on a Saturday or Sunday, where you can savor a new chapter for each of 24 weeks. This would allow you to try out your skills throughout the week before moving on to the next topic. **However you choose to move through the workbook, make sure to try something today, as a gift to yourself!**

Although the parts and chapters were designed to build upon each other, you can also do the exercises in any order you like. You can move though the workbook from start to finish starting with A Call to Adventure and the Three Good Things exercise in Chapter 1. Or you can skip around and go directly to the things you most want to use every day. Maybe right now you want to learn how to be more resilient (see Chapter 5) or you want to watch Maya Angelou talk about how Love Liberates (a personal favorite of mine) in Chapter 14.

You can see and hear Bruce Smith go through the lesson for each chapter in the **Author Videos**. These videos present the same lesson you can read about as the first part of each chapter of the workbook. The links to these videos are at the end of each chapter and there is also a complete list of them with all of their links in Appendix C. Although these Author Videos provide the same lesson that you can read in the chapter, these videos also have pictures to help illustrate the lessons and were also included in case you'd rather watch a video than read, or want to do both to reinforce or refresh yourself on the lessons.

If you choose to watch the Author Videos, you will notice that Bruce refers to each "day" of the challenge rather than each "chapter," and refers to each "week" of the challenge rather than each "part". This is because these videos were created for the initial four week challenge which this workbook grew out of. With 24 chapters in all, this meant finishing one chapter for the first six days of each week, followed by a day off before beginning the next week. **So, if you watch the Author Videos, remember to substitute "chapter" or "part" when Bruce talks about the "day" or "week" of the challenge.**

Each chapter in this workbook contains:

- **The lesson for the chapter.** The lesson is also covered in the Author Video listed at the end of each chapter.
- **A description of the chapter tasks.** There is a section at the end of each chapter that describes each of the tasks and why they were included.
- **The instructions for the chapter tasks.**
    - A link to the Author Video of the lesson for the chapter.
    - A link to an additional "Special Video" illustrating the topic for the chapter.
    - Positive psychology activities and questions to enable you to apply the chapter lesson and foster reflection and discussion with others.

This workbook is available as both a free PDF and a printed copy for the minimal no profit to us cost of approximately $6.00 on Amazon.com. Here is a link where you should be able to find it (you can also search on Amazon using the book title and author name):

https://www.amazon.com/Bruce-W-Smith/e/B078T27V58?ref=dbs_a_def_rwt_bibl_vu00_i0

Here is the link on our Center for Applied Positive Psychology website where you should be able to find the free PDF and download as many copies as you like:

https://drive.google.com/drive/folders/1eVPov4kbw-2WcYHU51Nbv8wi-aCC3y72?usp=sharing

This is also the link where we will make announcements about future online challenges, a discussion forum we are planning for those using this workbook, and where you may find a list of updated links if we find any of the links in the workbook stop working. If you have a printed copy, you may find it useful to get this list of links or down load the PDF copy of this workbook so that you will be able to click on the links.

If you have comments or questions or want to be on the list for future online challenges, please email us at the Center for Applied Positive Psychology at cappnmusa@gmail.com

Enjoy your journey through this positive psychology experience!

Honored to be a part of this project,

Tanya Kallan
Positive Psychology Enthusiast Cultivating My Best Life
Member of the Center for Applied Positive Psychology (CAPP)

Part 1 - Basic Training for Your Best Life

What is this part about?

Purpose: The purpose of this part is to enable you to better understand the kind of things that may make you most happy and how you can use this workbook to bring them more into your life.

Topics: There are chapters about what you most want in life, what will enable you to achieve it, and how to foster the mindfulness, resilience, wisdom, and creativity that will enable you do it.

Activities: The most important activities of this part focus on enabling you to better see, appreciate, and create more of the good things in your life that can bring you joy and happiness, despite whatever stress and challenges you may be dealing with.

Chapter 1

A Call to Adventure

Tell me, what is it you plan to do
with your one wild and precious life?
— Mary Oliver

Welcome to the positive psychology challenge! Through this workbook we are going to give you the opportunity to change your life through positive psychology. Positive psychology is the science of happiness and what makes life worth living.

This is no ordinary challenge focusing on only one area of your life, like flatter abs or the latest diet. Rather, this challenge can affect all areas of your life and what matters most. The big question that confronts us all was expressed in the words of the poet Mary Oliver: "Tell me, what is it you plan to do with your one wild and precious life?" The purpose of this challenge is to help you answer this question for yourself in the best way possible.

This challenge is sponsored by the Center for Applied Positive Psychology (CAPP) in New Mexico and is based on what was voted the best class at the University of New Mexico in Albuquerque, New Mexico. In addition, research has shown that the students who took this class have consistently had increased in happiness, well-being, and resilience and decreases in anxiety, depression, and stress - and this is one of our hopes for you!

Until recently, psychology had primarily focused on what goes wrong with people and reducing negative things like anxiety and depression. When Martin Seligman became the president of the American Psychological Association in 1998, he took the initiative to begin funding research on what makes us happy, what can go right with us, and how to foster them. This became what is now called positive psychology.

Our ancestors were able to survive because they paid enough attention to physical threats like spiders, snakes, and predators. However, we have inherited their tendency to focus on negative things that no longer threaten us and we continue to have such strong physical reactions to the daily hassles of life that it harms our mental and physical health. This bias toward the negative has kept us from seeing and fully appreciating some of the best things in our lives - things that bring us joy, meaning, and fulfillment and that can actually help us better cope with stress.

The purpose of positive psychology has been to enable us to rediscover and build on these things so that we can jump start our lives in moving toward the happiness and success that we seek. But don't let the word "positive" fool you, the positive in positive psychology does not mean that we have to deny that negative things happen in our lives. The positive in positive psychology means that it aims to help us move forward in a positive direction in the midst of, in spite, and sometimes even because of the stress that we experience and the bad things that happen to us.

In fact, we can think of how positive psychology can help us in the context of a "hero's journey" that involves facing our fears and learning from even some of the worst that happens as we seek to move towards a better life. The author and teacher Joseph Campbell studied stories around the world, across many centuries, and found the same stages in many of them, that these stages often reflect what happens in our lives, and that they can be used to inspire and guide us on our own journey.

Basically, there is a call to adventure into an unfamiliar place or unknown circumstances. The early part of the journey involves undergoing a series of smaller trials and tests, meeting people who can guide and mentor us, and learning the skills we need in order to face bigger challenges. Eventually, there comes a big test that involves confronting something particularly challenging or scary. Campbell says that "The cave you fear to enter, holds the treasure you seek." If the "hero" succeeds in learning, growing, and facing the greatest challenge, then they emerge transformed with rewards they could not have imagined and gifts that become just the kind of things that the rest of the world needs.

How is this kind of hero's journey related to the challenge of this workbook? This challenge is a call to adventure toward whatever you might want most and be best for you. Where does positive psychology come in? In our favorite stories there is often a mentor or guide like Obi-Wan and Yoda in *Star Wars* or Dumbledore in *Harry Potter* and often a power the hero needs to master, like the Force in *Star Wars* or magic in *Harry Potter.*

Positive psychology can help us in the same way by serving as a guide to show us the way and as a "force" that enables us to put what we learn into practice until we can fully embody it in the life we want. Thus, this positive psychology challenge is a call to the adventure of becoming our best and making the most of our lives - despite whatever stress, traumas, or bad things that we may experience along the way.

For each of the six chapters in the four parts of this challenge, you will have a lesson for the chapter, videos to illustrate it, activities and exercises to make it come alive, and the opportunity to reflect on and write about what you are learning. The lessons are grounded in positive psychology and related areas of science including neuroscience and other branches of psychology and the social sciences. Most important, research has shown that the activities and exercises you will be doing are effective in enabling people to increase their happiness and well-being and change their lives for the better.

In addition, each of the four parts build upon the previous part, with the first being basic training and identifying what may make you most happy, the second enabling you to identify and better use your strengths, the third empowering you to build better relationships and make a difference in the world around you, and the fourth in helping you prepare to build a better future beyond this challenge.

So, there are four parts, each with six chapters for a total of 24 chapters. While you can go at your own pace, we suggest that you get into a rhythm in doing a certain number of chapters every week. If you have time and really want to focus on a big change in a small amount of time, you could do one part or six chapters every week. If you did three chapters a week, the whole challenge would take eight weeks and if you did two chapters a week it would take 12 weeks.

If you were really busy and didn't have as much time, you could do one chapter a week which would take 24 weeks or close to six months. The other thing to keep in mind is that if you find a chapter that is particularly important to you, it may be good to spend more time on it and come back to it whenever you want or need to. Finally, the different parts and chapters have the kinds of lessons and activities that we can continue to learn and benefit from so you may want to go through them again at different times in your life.

Workbook Tasks for the Chapter

Now that you have answered this call to adventure and are ready to begin, let me tell you about the workbook tasks listed below for this chapter:

First, as you will find at the end of each chapter, there is a link for an "Author Video" where you can see and hear me going through the lesson for the chapter. Remember that the videos were originally created for a four week online challenge where people went through one chapter six days a week (with one day off) during four consecutive weeks. Thus, as you go at your own pace, just think about "chapters" or "parts" when you hear me talking about "days" or "weeks" in these videos.

Second, in order to help you better understand how you can benefit and increase your motivation for completing this workbook, there are reflection questions asking why you are doing this challenge and what you hope to gain from it.

Third, there is a link for a special video about Joseph Campbell's idea of a "hero's journey" for you to watch. This was included to help you understand how your life and this challenge might be like the kind of "hero's journey" that can motivate and inspire what you do in this challenge. You will be asked to write about the ways that your life has been like this kind of a hero's journey, how this challenge might be like a hero's journey for you, and what kind of an adventure this challenge might be calling you to.

Fourth, there is an activity that involves writing down three good things that happen in the next day. You will be doing a variation of this activity several times this during this first part of the challenge. We included this because it has been shown to be so effective in helping us reduce our bias towards the negative and see more of what is good around us. It also takes practice so it can be a good exercise to continue every day until it becomes a routine and natural part of your life.

Fifth, there is a well-being survey for you to complete and score. In the next chapter, we will help you understand the elements of well-being that the questions ask about on the survey. We include this survey at the end of the first and last chapter of this workbook so you can compare your scores and see what may have changed. The well-being survey is also included in Appendix E so you can make copies to use it at others times in order to see and think about how you are doing and compare your scores at different times.

1. Author Video of the Lesson

Here is the link for the video of me going over the lesson for this chapter.
https://youtu.be/rwYpX8ua8vs

2. Reflection Question

Why are you doing this challenge and what do you hope to gain from it?

3. Special Video – "What makes a hero? - Matthew Winkler"

Watch the video and think about how you can relate to the idea of a "hero's journey."

https://www.youtube.com/watch?v=Hhk4N9A0oCA&t=21s

In what way or ways has your life been like the kind of hero's journey described in the chapter and in the video?

____

____

____

____

____

____

____

____

____

____

____

____

In what ways or ways can this challenge be like this kind of hero's journey for you? What kind of adventure might it be calling you to?

____

____

4. Three Good Things Activity

Write down three good things that happen in the next day. They can be good in whatever way you define them and could be something you see, do, hear, or even just think about.

1.

2.

3.

5. Well-Being Survey

Instructions: First, circle the number that best indicates your response for each question. Second, add up your scores for the five elements of well-being (positive emotions, engagement, relationships, meaning, and accomplishment) and for negative emotions. Third, see what the scores mean in the table below and use this challenge to improve them.

1. In general, to what extent do you lead a purposeful and meaningful life?

   Not at all 0 1 2 3 4 5 6 7 8 9 10 Completely

2. How much of the time do you feel you are making progress towards accomplishing your goals?

   Never 0 1 2 3 4 5 6 7 8 9 10 Always

3. How often do you become absorbed in what you are doing?

   Never 0 1 2 3 4 5 6 7 8 9 10 Always

4. In general, how often do you feel joyful?

   Never 0 1 2 3 4 5 6 7 8 9 10 Always

5. To what extent do you receive help and support from others when you need it?

   Not at all 0 1 2 3 4 5 6 7 8 9 10 Completely

6. In general, how often do you feel anxious?

   Never 0 1 2 3 4 5 6 7 8 9 10 Always

7. How often do you achieve the important goals you have set for yourself?

   Never 0 1 2 3 4 5 6 7 8 9 10 Always

8. In general, to what extent do you feel that what you do in your life is valuable and worthwhile?

   Not at all 0 1 2 3 4 5 6 7 8 9 10 Completely

9. In general, how often do you feel positive?

   Never 0 1 2 3 4 5 6 7 8 9 10 Always

10. In general, to what extent do you feel excited and interested in things?

    Not at all 0 1 2 3 4 5 6 7 8 9 10 Completely

11. In general, how often do you feel angry?

    Never 0 1 2 3 4 5 6 7 8 9 10 Always

12. To what extent have you been feeling loved?

Not at all 0 1 2 3 4 5 6 7 8 9 10 Completely

13. How often are you able to handle your responsibilities?

Never 0 1 2 3 4 5 6 7 8 9 10 Always

14. To what extent do you generally feel you have a sense of direction in your life?

Not at all 0 1 2 3 4 5 6 7 8 9 10 Completely

15. How satisfied are you with your personal relationships?

Not at all 0 1 2 3 4 5 6 7 8 9 10 Completely

16. In general, how often do you feel sad?

Never 0 1 2 3 4 5 6 7 8 9 10 Always

17. How often do you lose track of time while doing something you enjoy?

Never 0 1 2 3 4 5 6 7 8 9 10 Always

18. In general, to what extent do you feel contented?

Not at all 0 1 2 3 4 5 6 7 8 9 10 Completely

Add up the total for each of the three questions for following:

_____ Positive Emotions (4, 9, 18)

_____ Engagement (3, 10, 17)

_____ Relationships (5, 12, 15)

_____ Meaning (1, 8, 14)

_____ Accomplishment (2, 7, 13)

_____ Negative Emotions (6, 11, 16)

Level of Well-Being	Ranges for Positive Emotions, Engagement, Relationships, Meaning & Accomplishment	Ranges for Negative Emotions
Very high	27-30	0-3
High	24-26	4-9
Average	20-23	10-15
Low	15-19	16-19
Very low	0-14	20-30

If you like, you can take the survey online and read more about it at the following address:

https://www.authentichappiness.sas.upenn.edu/questionnaires/perma

Chapter 2

What Do You Want Most?

Happiness is not a goal…
It's a by-product of a life well-lived.
— Eleanor Roosevelt

What do you want most in your life? Often people answer this question by listing the things that they think may make them happy. But what is happiness and what are the things that will make you happy?

Since positive psychology is the science of happiness and what makes life worth living, it may help us answer these questions for ourselves. First, happiness is not just about avoiding stress and the bad things that can happen to us because "stress happens" and will continue to happen. Positive psychology has shown that happiness is also about discovering and filling our lives with the good things that bring us pleasure, joy, meaning, and fulfillment. In the past, psychology focused primarily on avoiding negative things and emotions like anger, fear, and sadness; whereas positive psychology has focused much more on positive things and discovered the value of positive emotions like joy, love, interest, and contentment.

Second, the things that we think may make us happy may not always be the things that actually make us happy. Positive psychology has shown us that things like money, physical attractiveness, age, income, and IQ may not be as important as we thought and that things like time, optimism, self-esteem, having good friends, and meaningful ways to spend our time may be a lot more important than we thought. In fact, in her book *The Myths of Happiness*, Sonja Lyubormirsky shows us that it is possible to be happy when we may not have thought it possible – like when are single, older, without a lot of money, have serious health problems, or have experienced trauma or abuse.

Third, positive psychology has helped us discover a critical difference between the kind of good feeling or pleasure we may experience when we taste our favorite chocolate, on the one hand, and the lasting gratification we may get from being true to ourselves or trying to make the world a better place, on the other. The bottom line is that the things that we think may make us happy may not always do so and that the kind of happiness and well-being that we come to value the most may often involve more than just fleeting pleasure or the avoidance of negative emotions.

One of the most important theories in positive psychology is the one developed by its founder, Martin Seligman, about the things that may bring us lasting happiness and well-being. Seligman used the acronym PERMA where each of the five letters signify the five different things that we may seek for their own sake and that may us happy about our lives.

These five elements – along with negative emotions – were asked about in the survey that you were asked to complete at the end of the first chapter of this workbook.

As I go through each of the five elements of PERMA, I want you to think about which are most important to you and which you would most like to work on in this challenge. The P stands for positive emotions – like joy, interest, love, and contentment – and includes the pleasure that we often associate with happiness. Positive psychology has made many life-changing discoveries about the value of positive emotions. Barbara Fredrickson has shown that one of the reasons we have positive emotions is to enable us to broaden and build the strengths and resources we need for facing the challenges of life and better coping with stress. Jonathan Haidt has identified a positive emotion that he called "elevation," which is the warm, uplifting feeling we experience when we see unexpected acts of human goodness, kindness, or compassion and which can motivate us to act in the same way.

The E in PERMA stands for engagement – which refers to being absorbed, interested, and involved in an activity or the world itself. This kind of engagement includes the experience of flow – which was identified by one of the founders of the positive psychology movement – Mihaly Csikszentmihalyi – who has one of the hardest names to pronounce or spell that I know! We experience flow when we are so absorbed in something that we love to do, that we lose track of time and can do it for hours. Michael Jordan and LeBron James get into flow when they play basketball. For me it might be when I am teaching and for you it might be something else – like a sport, hobby, or some aspect of your work. But if we can find and continue to do things that put us into flow, we will increase the element of engagement and find ourselves feeling fulfilled and wanting to do it again and again.

The R in PERMA stands for relationships and refers to feeling loved, supported, and valued by others. Even if relationships aren't always pleasurable, we often seek them for their own sake. There are many popular songs about the pain we sometimes experience in our close relationships. There are many days when being a parent may not be pleasurable but we do it because we value our children and our relationships with them. Our brains and intelligence did not evolve to do calculus, read Shakespeare, or pass exams; but to understand and get along with other people – because they can be that important to us! One of the founders of positive psychology, Chris Peterson, summed it up in these three simple words, "Other people matter!"

The fourth letter in PERMA is M, which stands for meaning. This is having a sense of purpose and direction about where our life is going and the feeling that it is meaningful and worthwhile. It often includes being connected with something greater than ourselves, which could be spirituality or religion but could also be a movement, cause, nature, or the universe. Martin Seligman chose meaning for this theory because of the work of people like Viktor Frankl, who wrote a book called *Man's Search for Meaning.* In this book, Frankl talks about his experience in concentration camps in Nazi Germany during World War II. He believed that having a sense of meaning was the thing that enabled him to survive when so many around him were dying. There are many situations where a sense of meaning may be more important than pleasure, such as when we give ourselves to a cause that involves giving up some things we enjoy, or working hard in a challenging profession where the greatest rewards are in helping other people or improving the community.

The fifth and final letter in the acronym PERMA is A which stands for accomplishment – which involves achieving something and a sense of mastery. Sometimes we may do something for no other reason than that it brings us a sense of accomplishment and achievement. This could be getting the black belt that we may never need to use, finally getting that degree after years of being away from school, mastering that video game that no one else that we know understands, or climbing that mountain just because it is there.

These are the five kinds of things that we may seek for their own sake, for the satisfaction, gratification, reward, and – whether or not we understand why – just because we really want to! Remember the acronym PERMA - which stands for positive emotions, engagement, relationships, meaning, and accomplishment. Which of these are most important to you? Which would you most like to work on and increase in this challenge?

Workbook Tasks for the Chapter

The tasks for chapter will help you answer these questions and begin a practice that can help you see and appreciate more of the good things that happen all around you.

First, as after every chapter, there is a link to an Author Video where you can see and hear me going over the lesson for this chapter.

Second, there is a link for a special video by Alan Watts where he asks the question "What do you desire?" This is another way of asking Mary Oliver's question about what you plan to do with your "one wild and precious life." After watching the video, think about what it is that you most desire and want for your life.

Third, there is a variation of the three good things activity that you did in the last chapter and will help you continue to see more of the positive and good things in your life. This time we want you to review your list at the end of the day and reflect on the three things you identified before you go to bed. This will help you remember and recall them so they might be more present to you during different times of the day in the future.

Fourth, there are 10 questions that will help you determine what may bring you the greatest happiness and what may be most important for you to focus on in this challenge. These questions are based on a variety of valuable exercises used by counselors, personal coaches, trainers, and teachers to enable people to determine what may be the best goals for them to work towards.

Fifth, there are questions for you to reflect on and answer to help you decide which of the five elements of PERMA that we talked about in this chapter are most important to you and which ones you may most want to work on.

1. Author's Video of the Lesson

Here is the link for the video of me going over the lesson for this chapter.

https://youtu.be/ccM094t4Cas

2. Special Video - "Alan Watts - What Do You desire?"

Watch the following video and think about what you desire or want most in your life.

https://www.youtube.com/watch?v=JCUFs2qJ1bs

3. Three Good Things Activity

Write down three good things that happen in the next day. Before the end of the day, read the list to remind yourself of them and reflect on them before you go to bed.

1. ______________________________

____

2. ______________________________

____

3. ______________________________

____

4. Happiness Questions

Answer these questions and think about what you want most out of this challenge:

1. What has brought you the most happiness in the past?

____

____

____

____

____

____

2. What do you think would bring you the most happiness in the future?

3. Who are the most important people in your life?

4. What do you like to do in your spare time?

5. What would you most like to do for work?

6. What has brought the most meaning to your life?

7. What are your most important goals for the future?

8. What would you do if you had all the time and money in the world?

9. How would you like to be remembered after you are gone?

10. What do you most want out of life?

5. Reflection Questions

What element or elements of PERMA are most important to you? Why?

What element(s) of PERMA would you most like to work on in this challenge? Why?

Chapter 3

How Can You Make It Happen?

Follow your bliss and the universe will open doors for you where there were only walls.
—Joseph Campbell

How can you create the kind of life that you want most? What can enable you to achieve your goals and reach the destination you see for yourself on your own "hero's journey"?

In the first chapter, we talked about the call to adventure. In the second chapter, we asked you to think about what you want most in your life and most out of this challenge. In this chapter, we will introduce three building blocks of positive change that can go a long way in making that happen and that you'll have the chance to bring to life in this challenge.

The first is something that is a part of the cognitive therapy that helps people overcome depression and also something you can see in Walt Disney, J.K. Rowling, and Steve Jobs and in the greatest inventions and most beautiful visions of the future. It is in the power that we possess to think about things in a new way – and it is called positive reappraisal. It is the ability to change our minds to see things in a way that is more beneficial and useful.

Near the beginning of the first chapter, I talked about how humans evolved to have a negativity bias because our ancestors paid more attention to negative things like lions, tigers, and bears. In addition, it turns out that we also have the capacity to reappraise things in a positive way that can reduce this bias and enable us to more fully see, appreciate, and enjoy the good things around us.

By simply noting three good things like you did after the first two chapters and will continue to do after this chapter and the next, you are learning to exercise your power to see the world in a new and different way. Rather than calling it positive reappraisal – we might simply call it the power to change our minds and our perspective to see more of what is good or beautiful, and what bring us joy and happiness now and in the future.

So, the first building block of positive change is positive reappraisal – our ability to change our minds for the better. The second has more to do with what we do than what we think. It too has been very effective in helping people overcome depression. But until recently it was almost entirely neglected in enabling people to become their best and helping them reach the heights of joy, meaning, and success. It is all too easy to overlook or forget.

It too has been a driving force for some of the most successful people and greatest achievements in art, music, science, literature, and sports. It has to do with finding those little things that you - and maybe only you - love to do. These include things that you could do for hours at a time, things that your friends and family members may not understand at all, and may even think you are a little strange for doing. They are so easy to miss when we are busy doing what we think we should rather than what we really want to do.

The technical name for this is "behavioral activation" because it has been a way to get people who are depressed to begin to be active and involved with life again. In fact, research has showed that once many of them have started to do this, they often begin to experience pleasure again, and don't want to quit! Behavioral activation is everywhere in positive psychology – and is big part of many of the exercises that you will be doing. Joseph Campbell called it "following your bliss" – which means to do those things that you love to do and that you feel like you were made and meant to do.

The idea of behavioral activation is to find things that you enjoy doing so much that you don't want to stop and that they help you find what you love to do, what you might get paid well to do, and what often brings you to other people who also love to do it. This frequently the element of Engagement in PERMA and the experience of flow, which is like being in the zone that athletes get into when they are at the top of their game.

So, the first thing is positive reappraisal, the ability to change our minds for the better, and the second is behavioral activation, the power of doing things that you really love to do. But, as they said in *Star Wars*, "there is another" and this other can be most clearly seen in the most challenging part of that "hero's journey" that we can see in *Star Wars*, in other popular and inspiring movies and stories, and in the story of our lives.

We can see this power most clearly in the "exposure" therapies that enable us to overcome anxiety and face the things that we fear the most. This can also be one of the greatest sources of courage and best ways to increase it. Some of us may think that courage means not feeling fear, but the reason why exposure therapies work is that they provide a supportive context for gradually exposing ourselves to what we are afraid of.

When we are really afraid of something, our strongest inclination is usually just avoid it. If we are terrified of public speaking, then we may not take a job or class where we have to speak much in front of other people. If we are afraid of being rejected, we may avoid dating or trying to make new friends. If we have a fear of failure, we may avoid trying something new or something that we are not sure that we can do well. But when we avoid doing what we are afraid of, our fear grows and we don't have the chance to learn that we can reduce it.

Whereas when we face it and move forward anyway, we generally discover that the fear begins to melt away and we gain increased confidence in our ability to overcome our fears. This is how this third principle of exposing ourselves to what we fear helps us. In facing the things you might be afraid of in this challenge, exposing yourself to what you are afraid is often what it takes to defeat the inner "dragons" we may fear the most. For most of us at most times, courage may not be the absence of fear, but finding a way to go forward in spite of it – just as this challenge is designed to enable you to move forward in spite of stress.

There are two things that may help us in exposing ourselves to what we are afraid of rather than just continuing to avoid it. The first is that we can often gradually expose ourselves to what we are afraid of so we can gain more courage and confidence before facing our greatest fears. The second is that although there is no one else who can face our fears for us, there are friends, mentors, and fellow travelers who can encourage and support us as we do it and who may even face some of the same fears with us.

But we can also get help from the first two building blocks and all three can begin to work together for us. When you can change your mind using positive reappraisal, you can better see the gifts and rewards that you may get for facing your fears and begin to see yourself as having the courage that it takes. When you can get a taste of those things that you love to do in using behavioral activation – even when you are sick or tired or scared - the motivation to act will often become greater than the fear that holds you back.

As you go through this challenge, you may not always be aware you are doing it, but you will often have the opportunity to practice these three building blocks. You will be using positive reappraisal to see things in a more beneficial light, behavioral activation to identify and practice doing more of the things you love do, and exposing yourself to what you fear to build the confidence and courage you need. The more you are aware of and practice these keys to positive change, the more you will be like that Jedi master in *Star Wars* who learns to use the power of the Force. Although many people are not aware of them, research has consistently shown they can be a potent force in our lives - which can not only can free us from anxiety and depression but can enable us to make the most of our lives.

Workbook Tasks for the Chapter

With these building blocks in mind, here are the tasks that will help you understand, appreciate, and benefit from them.

First, as after every chapter, there is a link to a video where you can see and hear me going over the lesson for this chapter.

Second, there is special TED talk video with Shawn Achor talking about the value of positive psychology and how happiness can lead to success. You will see him give an example where positive reappraisal helped his sister cope with an injury and you will see him talk about the benefits of many of the activities you will be doing in this challenge.

Third, you will once again be asked to write down three good things that happen to you in the next day. This time we want you to reflect on them before you go to bed and also try to think of where you may see good things during the coming week. This will help you practice positive reappraisal and enable you to change how you see the world around you.

Fourth, you will have a list of pleasant activities and you will be asked to identify the top 10 that you would like to try. This task is a form of behavioral activation that can help you discover new things that you may enjoy doing and want to make more a part of your life.

Finally, there are reflection questions about what new pleasant event you would most like to try and also about what fears you might need to face on your way to getting the most out of life. This may help you see how you can use things you love to do as a motivation and reward for exposing yourself to things you are afraid of and that get in the way of your living the kind of life you most want.

1. Author Video of the Lesson

Here is the link for the video of me going over the lesson for this chapter.

https://youtu.be/8ZDDcz5D5Vo

2. Special Video - "Shawn Achor - The Happiness Advantage"

Watch the video and think about how focusing on your own happiness may lead to success in different areas of your life. Also, look for when he talks about his sister the "unicorn" and how you could use your imagination in a similar way to cope with a stressful or challenging time.

https://www.youtube.com/watch?v=GXy__kBVq1M

3. Three Good Things Activity

First, write down three good things that happen during the next day. Second, read the list and reflect on them before you go to bed. Finally, take a few minutes to think about when and where you might see these and other kinds of good things during the next week or two.

1. ______________________________

____

2. ______________________________

____

3. ______________________________

____

4. Pleasant Events Activity

Read the list of pleasant events (see Appendix F), list the top 10 that you would like to try below, and rank them from 1 to 10 with #1 being the one you most want to try.

____

____

Which of the pleasant activities that you listed would you like to try in the next week? When and where could you try it?

What happened when you tried the pleasant event that you planned to do? How do you think it affected you?

5. Reflection Questions

What are you afraid of that may get in the way of getting what you want out of life?

____

____

____

____

____

What kind of rewards might make exposing yourself to what you are afraid of worth it?

____

____

____

____

____

How can you use positive reappraisal or behavioral activation to you move forward in spite of your fears?

____

____

____

____

____

Chapter 4

Mindfulness and Acceptance

Mindfulness is a way of befriending ourselves and our experience.
— Jon Kabat-Zinn

So far you have learned about this positive psychology challenge as a call to an adventure. It is the adventure of moving closer towards the kind of life that you want most. This could involve increasing the elements of PERMA - positive emotions, engagement, relationships, meaning, and accomplishment - or some other goals or things you think may bring you greater happiness and well-being.

In the last chapter, you learned about three building blocks that you will use throughout this challenge and that will make your adventure and positive changes in your life possible. Positive reappraisal is the ability to change your mind to see more good things and how your life can be better, behavioral activation involves finding and doing more of what you enjoy and may really love to do, and exposing yourself to what you are afraid will enable you to build the courage you need to face and overcome your greatest fears and obstacles.

In this chapter, I want to say something about the best place to start with this and any journey, and that is right here and right now – with practicing mindfulness and acceptance. The psychologist Carl Rogers once said, "The curious paradox is that when I accept myself just as I am, then I can change." Mindfulness is about accepting where you are right here and now, so that the changes that you want and need in your life can begin to happen.

Mindfulness was first introduced to many people in the Western world 30-40 years ago by a then young scientist named Jon Kabat-Zinn who had studied it in Buddhism. He developed a program to use mindfulness to help people with anxiety, stress, and chronic pain that doctors had not been very successful in treating. Kabat-Zinn has defined mindfulness as "paying attention in a particular way: on purpose in the present moment, and non-judgmentally."

So, mindfulness is the awareness of what is happening right now, within us and around us. It involves focusing our attention on this in the present moment and continuing to do this moment by moment. And it involves the open and accepting observation of "what is" right now without any attempt to judge whether it is right or wrong or good or bad. When we can see and fully take in what is happening right now, we can understand where we are and can begin to move forward and make the changes that may be important for us.

You can see mindfulness in many famous teachers – going back to Buddha himself, in the modern Buddhist teacher Thich Nhat Hanh, and in Eckhart Tolle who wrote a book called *The Power of Now*. Mindfulness has become an important part of positive psychology in that it enables us to fully notice, take in, and appreciate the good things in our lives that we may otherwise miss.

Mindfulness can also play a critical role in enabling us to perform and function at our best. George Mumford is a former professional basketball player who has taught people like Phil Jackson, Michael Jordan, and Kobe Bryant to use mindfulness to reach the top of their game. Mumford wrote a book called *The Mindful Athlete* that is not only good for athletes but for all of us who want to be at our best. Ryan Niemiec is psychologist who has used mindfulness to enable people to better focus on and use their strengths. He wrote a book called *Mindfulness and Character Strengths* that presents a program for how we can practice mindfulness to better see, appreciate, and use the best in ourselves.

There are many ways that you can begin to benefit from mindfulness. You can read a book by someone like Jon Kabat-Zinn, George Mumford, or Ryan Niemiec. You can take the Mindfulness-Based Stress Reduction course, also known as MBSR, developed by Jon Kabat-Zinn and is now being regularly taught on the internet and in most major cities.

To help you get started in benefitting from mindfulness, I want to do two things in the rest of this chapter. First, I want to make you aware of two common barriers to practicing mindfulness. Second, I want to tell you about four ways that you can begin to practice. In addition, we will give you the opportunity to practice a form of mindfulness for one of the activities listed at the end of this chapter.

The first common barrier to mindfulness is that we spend so much time focusing on the past or the future that, at first, it can seem nearly impossible for some of us to focus on the present. It is important for us to try to learn from our past and plan for the future, but if we are never fully aware of and attentive to the present, we may not be able to show up for and really experience and live our lives.

The second common barrier is that we are constantly judging and evaluating whether what we are thinking and feeling is useful or good, and whether what is happening around us bodes ill or well for us. Mindfulness not only involves letting go of the past and the future, but also letting go of our judgments about them which frees us to be more open to fully experiencing our lives in the present.

If you try to practice mindfulness, be gentle, patient, and kind with yourself when judgments and thoughts of the past or future come up. It is easy to react to one judgment with more judgment, whereas it is may be more beneficial just to note that you are making a judgment and simply return your focus to your experience in the present.

With these common potential barriers in mind, here are four ways that you can begin to practice mindfulness.

The first way is called mindful breathing where you focus on your breath as it goes in and out of your body. You can focus on your breath wherever you are most aware of it - your nose, your chest, or your abdomen as it rises and falls. This also may be a simple and effective way for you to learn to relax wherever they are.

The second way is practice mindfulness is called a body scan where you focus on the sensations in different parts of your body. It usually begins with your feet and gradually moves up through your whole body to your head and face. This is particularly helpful for those of us who have recurrent pain in different parts of our bodies. What many like this find in doing the body scan is that the pain is often not as bad as they feared and that it comes and goes much more than always being there as a constant pain.

The third way to practice mindfulness is called choiceless awareness where you practice allowing your attention to go wherever it goes and wherever it is drawn. This is harder than it may sound because we are so easily distracted by thoughts of the past, the future, judgments about how we are doing, and thinking about where we should focus our attention.

The fourth way to practice mindfulness simply involves being more mindful during the regular activities of daily living such as walking, washing dishes, cleaning the house, gardening, or any simple repetitive activity. While many people may need quiet times free of distraction to begin to learn to focus mindfully on the present, this practicing of mindful awareness during daily activities can be a way to bring mindfulness more into everyday life.

So the lesson for this chapter is about the power of mindfulness in making acceptance possible and the value of being fully present to our lives. Mindfulness involves paying full attention to and having a full awareness of our lives in the present. It enables us to accept "what is" so that we can fully appreciate, enjoy, and savor it, and also begin to make whatever changes may be important for enabling us to move forward on our journeys.

Workbook Tasks for the Chapter

The tasks for this chapter are all designed to enable you to more fully understand and experience mindfulness and the mindful acceptance of the present.

First, as after every chapter, there is a link to a video where you can see and hear me going over the lesson for this chapter.

Second, there is a link for a special video about the kind of thing that mindfulness will enable us to see and more fully appreciate, and how joy can break into our lives when we least expect it!

Third, there is a guided mindful breathing exercise that will help you to begin to practice and experience mindfulness. There is a link below for a website where you can find this and other guided mindfulness meditations and practices such as the body scan presented above.

Fourth, there is again the opportunity to write down three good things that happen during the coming day. But this time you are also asked to read the list and reflect on them before the end of your day and write about how you can use mindfulness to appreciate at least one of them more in the future.

Fifth, there are reflection questions about how mindfulness might benefit you in your life and about what has helped you the most in relaxing and what might best help you relax in the future.

1. Author Video for the Lesson

Here is the link for the video of me going over the lesson for this chapter.

https://youtu.be/S_dAoCZe-W4

2. Special Video - "Flashmob – Ode an die Freude (Ode to Joy)"

Watch the video and think about where and how you could be more open to joy in your life and think about the potential sources of joy and happiness that you would like to pay more attention to.

https://www.youtube.com/watch?v=kbJcQYVtZMo

3. Mindful Breathing Activity

Go to following link:

https://www.uclahealth.org/marc/mindful-meditations

Do the Breathing Exercise (5 minutes) and any of the other meditations you'd like to try.

4. Three Good Things Activity

Write down three good things that happen in the next day. Before you go to bed, read the list and reflect on each of them and then write a about how you could use mindfulness to appreciate one of them more in the future.

1. ____

____

2. ____

____

3. ____

____

How I can use mindfulness to appreciate one of these things more in the future:

____

5. Reflection Questions

How might mindfulness benefit or help you in your life?

What are the ways that you have found to be most helpful in relaxing? Which one do you think would be most helpful for the future?

How could you make what would be most helpful more a part of your normal routine?

Chapter 5

Resilience and Stress-Related Growth

Do not judge me by my success,
judge me by how many times
I fell down and got back up again.
— Nelson Mandela

We have now begun a journey towards the kind of life we most want for ourselves. In Chapter 2, we learned about the kinds of things we might want to aim for to increase our happiness and well-being. In Chapter 3, we learned about positive reappraisal as our ability to see our lives in a new and better light, behavioral activation as a way to find and focus more on things that we love to do, and gradually exposing ourselves to the things we fear as a way to build courage. In the last chapter, we learned about how mindfulness can enable us to be present and accept where we are so that we can really begin to move forward.

The purpose of this chapter is to focus on what we can do when the inevitable things happen that cause use stress and get in our way. There are probably few realities that become more apparent to us as we go through life than the fact that "stress happens."

Yet there are also few things that we admire more in others than the capacity to be resilient in bouncing back and even learning and growing from stress. This is where positive psychology has shown through the dark clouds like the sun after a long rainy season. If you only paid attention to clinical or abnormal psychology, with their focus on what goes wrong with us, you might think that resilience was a rare thing.

But in recent times, psychologists like George Bonanno have shown that even when people experience traumatic events, only about one out of four develop posttraumatic stress disorder (PTSD) and as many as one half experience something you may not have even heard of – "posttraumatic growth," which has also simply been called "stress-related growth." Posttraumatic or stress-related growth refers to the learning, growth, and benefits that can result from the traumatic and stressful experiences we have in our lives.

Another great thing that psychology has discovered in the past 20-30 years is that there is so much that we can do to increase our resilience and also our ability to learn, grow, and benefit from the stress in our lives. Let's start with the things we can do to increase our resilience.

The first harkens back to the lesson in the previous chapter about mindfulness and the other five things we will mention will also be a focus in later chapters of this workbook. When stress happens, our sympathetic nervous system has evolved to quickly put us into the "fight or flight response" where we may hastily act out of anger or fear. Mindfulness can interrupt this initial knee-jerk reaction to a stressful event. It can give us time to pause and more fully take in and assess the situation and then think about how best to respond rather than just simply react.

The second thing that can help us increase resilience is positive reappraisal - thinking about a stressful situation in new and more positive and potentially beneficial light. Once we pause and begin to think about how we want to respond, we can challenge our fears about the worst happening, envision ourselves as being resilient, and begin to discover new more constructive ways to cope.

The third thing we can do to increase resilience is simply to not give up when a goal is really important to us. We will talk more about this in our lesson on perseverance and grit in the second part of this workbook. But at the end of this chapter, there is a link to a dramatic and memorable example of this in a young woman who embodies resilience when the worst happens while she is running in a big race during an indoor track meet.

The fourth way to increase resilience is by increasing what is called "self-efficacy," which is the belief that we can do what it takes to bounce back and be resilient. We will have a whole lesson in the second part of this workbook about self-efficacy. During this upcoming lesson, we will give you the five well-established ways that you can increase your self-efficacy for resilience or for achieving any other important goal that you might have.

The fifth way to increase resilience involves a having a sense of meaning or purpose in life. This is illustrated in the life of Viktor Frankl, whose strong sense of meaning and purpose enabled him to survive four concentration camps during World War II in Nazi Germany. When you have something to live for, someone who depends on you, or a reason to keep going on and living; you are much more likely to prevail during stressful times.

Finally, just as there is strength in numbers, so there is also resilience in numbers. Social support is the psychological term for having people to count on when we are under stress and really need them. Social support in the form of friends, family, a team, a work group, a church, or the larger community can play a critical role in resilience. We might reverse the familiar saying to make it – "Divided we fall and united we stand!"

So, these are some of the primary ways that we can foster resilience:

1. Mindfulness, which involves pausing to assess the situation and think about how to best respond.

2. Positive reappraisal, which involves seeing ourselves as resilient and finding ways to cope that enable us to bounce back.

3. Perseverance, which means simply not giving up when something is really important to us.

4. Self-efficacy, which is the belief that we have what it takes to be resilient.

5. Meaning and purpose, which involves having something that is worth living or a reason for being resilient.

6. Social support, which means having people we can count on in times of stress and reaching out and allowing them to help us when we need it.

What about posttraumatic or stress-related growth – which is not just bouncing back but learning, growing, and benefitting from stress? What can enable us to make this happen or at least more likely when we are under stress? First, it may help just to be aware of the different kinds of benefits that people report coming from stressful events so we can begin to look for them and believe that they may be possible for us. These benefits have included:

1. Finding new opportunities and possibilities
2. Becoming a stronger person
3. Having improved personal relationships
4. Making new friends
5. Developing a greater appreciation of life
6. Developing a greater sense of meaning and purpose
7. Spiritual growth

In addition to being aware of the different kinds of growth or benefits that are possible, there are other things we can do to foster them. The first is something we have already talked about in relation to resilience: positive reappraisal. You remember that positive reappraisal involves changing your mind to see things in a new way that may be more beneficial to us now or in the future. So even when the worst happens, positive reappraisal involves daring to think about a stressful situation in a new way and being open to how you might learn, grow, or benefit from it.

The second way to foster stress-related growth is to think about our stress in the context of the kind of hero's journey that Joseph Campbell wrote about and you learned about in Chapter 1. The stages of the hero's journey not only include facing our greatest fear, but also gaining a reward or benefit as we emerge on the other side of fighting our scariest dragons. Many people have drawn inspiration from stories of people like Jesus or Buddha because they were reborn or grew to a higher level of existence after death or a dark night.

The third way to increase stress-related growth is to talk or write about our experience with stress or trauma while keeping positive reappraisal and the potential rewards of a hero's journey in mind. This can involve sharing the experience with a trusted friend, counselor, or mentor who can help us learn, grow, and find benefits. This can also be done by writing about the experience in the context of a story that inspires us or where we just begin to brainstorm about the ways we may be able to learn or grow from the experience.

Thus, the lesson for this chapter is a basic and critical one for all of us. It is the good news about the possibility of resilience and stress-related growth and how to foster them. These are two of our greatest weapons in the face of the inevitable stress that will get in our way. They are also two of the greatest gifts for enabling us to move from only surviving to thriving and making the most of our lives.

Resilience enables us to get back to our previous level of happiness and well-being and maintain it in the midst of stress.

Stress-related growth enables us to go above and beyond making it possible to gain something from the experience and, as we see in the final stage of the hero's journey, offer it back to the world so that others can also benefit.

Yes, "stress happens," and will undoubtedly continue to happen in our lives. The good news is that we are learning so much about the capacity we all have to bounce back and make it the very occasion for us to become our best and live our lives to the fullest.

I began the first chapter quoting Mary Oliver's question asking us "what we plan to do with our one wild and precious life?" The "wild" part may have something to do with the stress that will continue to challenge us while the "precious" part may be what we have the opportunity to bring to life when the wild things come out.

Stay tuned! There is much more about this to come!

Workbook Tasks for the Chapter

With these in mind, here are some things you can do to foster resilience and stress-related growth and enable you to see and create more good things that happen around you every day:

First, as after every chapter, there is a link to a video where you can see and hear me going over the lesson for this chapter.

Second, there is a video of an extraordinary example of resilience in the life of a young woman. When I have shown this video to a large class, there are often audible gasps and tears in the eyes of the students as they see what she did when the worst happened. After you watch the video, reflect on your reaction and see if you can think of times in your life when you may have responded in a similar way.

The third and fourth tasks involve writing about a time that you were resilient in the past and about a time you might need to be resilient in the future. This may seem like a simple exercise that only involves answering questions about your own experience. However, research has shown that taking the time to freely and thoughtfully write about this often helps people better cope with stress and improve their happiness and well-being.

The more you reflect on when you have been resilient in the past, the more you increase your confidence to be resilient in the future and remember to do the things that may help you be more resilient. The more you reflect on when you may have to be resilient in the future, the more you will be confident and ready when the time comes.

Fifth, the last task again involves writing down three good things that happen in the next day. But this time, you are also asked to write about how you can make at least one of the three good things happen more in the future. This will not only help you discover what you can do to make more good things happen, it will also make you less likely to miss them and be more aware of and ready to appreciate them.

1. Author Video for this Lesson

Here is the link for the video of me going over the lesson for this chapter.

https://youtu.be/2dndl9JI51E

2. Special Video - "Heather Dorniden's Inspiring 600 meter race"

Watch the video and think of what it might look like for you to respond in the same way to some of the challenges that you may face in the future.

https://www.youtube.com/watch?v=70UF82nysIU

3. Resilience in the Past

What is a time that you were resilient and what enabled you to bounce back? Be as thoughtful and free as you can in expressing your thoughts and feelings about the experience and what may have helped you.

___

___

___

___

___

___

___

___

___

___

___

4. Resilience in the Future

Write about a time that you may have to be resilient in the future and what might help you be resilient. Be as thoughtful and free as you can in expressing your thoughts and feelings about what you think you may experience and what may help you be resilient.

5. Three Good Things Activity

Write down three good things that happen in the next day and then write about how you can make at least one of them happen more in the future.

1.

2.

3.

How I can make at least one of these good things happen more in the future?

Chapter 6

Wisdom and Creativity

Happiness can be found, even in the darkest of times,
if one only remembers to turn on the light.

— Albus Dumbledore

Congratulations, we are coming to the end of the first part of the positive psychology challenge in this workbook! We hope you will take any time you need to rest, rejuvenate, and reward yourself for what you have accomplished so far. In the second part of this challenge, we will focus on helping you identify, build, and use your strengths and what is best in you. In the third part, we will focus on enabling you to improve your relationships and your ability to be involved with and impact the larger community and world around you. Finally, in the fourth part, we will focus on enabling you to create a master plan for the kind of life that you might want most and might make you most happy in the future.

There is one more basic lesson in this chapter that will help you plot your course and find your way during the rest of this challenge. We want to talk about how you can foster two things that have been thought to be important for centuries, but that most people think there is little they can do to foster in themselves. The first is wisdom and the second is creativity.

What is wisdom and why might it be so important for our lives and this challenge? Simply put, wisdom is not just intelligence or what we can learn in school. It is the practical knowledge that comes from life experience and enables us to achieve the happiness, well-being, and success we seek in everyday life. It enables us to live in a world of uncertainty, where there are so many different kinds of people, and where so much is relative, changing, and depends on the situation and context.

One common example of wisdom is in what is called *The Serenity Prayer* – that asks for the courage to change what we can, the serenity to accept what we can't change, and the wisdom to know the difference.

Another example of wisdom that the psychologist Barry Schwartz has provided has to do with how we make decisions. There are some people that he calls "maximizers" who always try to consider every alternative before making a decision. There are others he calls "satisficers" who only look until they find an alternative or option that is good enough. It turns out that there are some situations where it may be better to be a maximizer and other situations, in a world of so many options, where we may be happier if we just go with what is good enough. Again, the wisdom may be in knowing the difference!

How might wisdom help you in this challenge? For one thing, it may help you decide what is most important to work on, what element of PERMA you might most want to increase, and what goals you might best have for the future. For one of your activities for this chapter, we are going to give you a task that will help increase your wisdom about your life by giving your more perspective on what you may want to work on and try to improve. But for now, let me tell about what we have learned about how we can foster wisdom in our lives.

First, we can learn from the wise people that we may know by asking them our toughest questions - or even asking them to become a mentor for us.

Second, we can learn from wise people in history by watching documentaries and reading about them, especially those we admire and who have faced challenges that may be similar to our own.

Third, we can become more aware of our own wisdom by having a dialogue with a real or fictional wise person. In doing this, we may realize that – like Dorothy in the Wizard of Oz – some of what we seek may already lie within us.

Fourth, many people find it useful to 'google' lists of quotes from wise people, identify the ones that they resonate with the most, reflect on how and why these quotes speak to them, and then use them as a guide in making tough decisions.

Fifth, we can make it a point to get to know people who have different perspectives and experiences from our own. Einstein said that "Problems cannot be solved with the same mindset that created them" and we may need to look for and put ourselves into a different mindset to solve a challenging problem.

Sixth, we can become a mentor, guide, or teacher for someone else. You may be surprised by what you already know and don't know - and with what you might learn in the process of trying to teach someone else.

But even more than with wisdom, many people think that creativity is just not in the cards for them. Like them, you may think that you are just not a creative person. It turns out that this may more often be an excuse than the truth. Creativity has been defined simply as a new way to think about, see, or do something that serves some adaptive or constructive function or purpose.

The problem is that most of us think of creativity only in terms of the rare things that people like Leonardo Da Vinci or Albert Einstein have done that changed the world. In contrast, creativity researchers have found that we all have a remarkable aptitude for creativity where it counts – in the uniqueness of our own everyday lives and in the specific challenges that we face.

I remember talking to an older student who was down on herself because she didn't think she was creative enough to be an artist. As she talked, I realized that creativity and art were readily apparent in the picture she was painting with her whole life. It was obvious in the way that she balanced her conflicting demands, worked at night, took a full load of classes, found parking in time to get to class, did a great job raising her children, and later in the way that she wove all of her experiences together in using them to help her reach her goal of getting a graduate degree and becoming a licensed professional counselor.

The reality is that human beings have evolved to become inherently creative, especially when we are living out own lives and not trying to live those of someone else. But even more important, research has shown there are many things we can all do to foster creativity.

First, we can simply give ourselves time to brainstorm by making lists – like were you asked to do for the pleasant events activity earlier in this first part of our challenge, or will be asked to do in finding new ways to use your strengths in the next part.

Second, we can get together with a friend or group of friends who can help us get started in brainstorming and coming up with new ideas, if we have trouble starting on our own.

Third, we can practice mindfulness by paying attention to our senses, whatever is happening right now, and take notice of the new things we may not have seen before.

Fourth, as with the behavioral activation we talked about and the pleasant events list you reviewed, you can try all kinds of different things and continue to do the things you enjoy the most. The positive emotions that doing pleasant activities cause have consistently been shown to be a source of creativity. When we are feeling good, we are more likely to feel the freedom to think about new things than when we are feeling down and only focusing on one negative thing that has happened or that we are afraid might happen.

Fifth, we can find new ways to experience flow and do them as much as we can. Flow is fertile ground for creativity because the more we do something, the better we get at it, and the more likely we will be to discover new and better ways to do it.

Sixth, we can redecorate a room or a part of a room where we live or work in a way that that says something unique about us. When we are free to make something our own, we are naturally more likely to think of new ideas and approaches that reflect our own uniqueness.

Yes, the reality is that there is no one else just like you - your experience and perspective are unique. You can paint a picture with your life that has a beauty all its own that no one else can match. During this challenge, we hope that you will do some of these things to foster your inherent capacity for wisdom and creativity and that you will use them to get a clearer picture of where you want to go in your life and how you can get there.

Workbook Tasks for the Chapter

Here are the tasks that can foster your wisdom in understanding how balanced your life is and your creativity in benefiting from stress and in noticing the good things in your life.

First, as after every chapter, there is a link to a video where you can see and hear me going over the lesson for this chapter.

Second, there is a video where a woman displays her creativity in finding benefits in something no one would want. We wanted to give you an example of the kinds of benefits you might be able to find after some of the worst things you could think of happen to you.

Third, there are reflection questions asking you to write about a time that something good came out of something bad and how something good might come out of something stressful you are currently dealing with. This is a way of fostering wisdom and creativity where it matters most - when we are facing a challenging or stressful situation. In addition, as with the activity in Chapter 5 where you wrote about a time you were resilient, research has shown that writing about when you have benefited from stress helps you better cope with stress, improve your happiness and well-being, and experience stress-related growth.

Fourth, there is an activity called the "wheel of life" to help increase your wisdom in grasping the big picture of your life. This task involves rating how satisfied you are in different areas of your life and then thinking about and identifying the areas that you would most like to work on. There is a link to a website that can make this a quick and easy way to get an overview of how satisfied you are with the important aspects of your life.

Finally, although we hope you will continue to note the good things that happen to you during the day in the future, for the last time we are asking you to do a variation of these simple but potentially powerful task. We began with this activity in this first part of the challenge because so many people have found it helpful in reducing their bias toward the negative and in taking on a new perspective on their lives.

Thus, this time the task involves both noting three good things and thinking about how you might continue to benefit from an exercise like this by making it a part of your regular routine. For example, you may want to continue to do it every day for the rest of the challenge, do it weekly or a few days a week, or identify a different number of good things every day. In addition, you could focus on different kinds of good things like those you see in your friends and family members, good things that happen in your school or work life, or those that are beautiful, funny, or meaningful in some way.

Beyond that, we hope that you will take time to appreciate and celebrate what you have done in the first part of this challenge!

1. Author Video for the Lesson

Here is the link for the video of me going over the lesson for this chapter.

https://youtu.be/BYyAVCBnEqE

2. Special Video - "The best gift I ever survived | Stacey Kramer"

Watch the video and think about how you may have benefited or may benefit when something bad has happened to you.

https://www.youtube.com/watch?v=LgTnmWZX39w

3. Reflection Questions

Write about a time something good came out of something stressful, negative, or bad.

____

Write about how something good might come out of something stressful, negative, or bad that you are currently dealing with. It might help to review the bullet list of the different kinds of benefits people have reported that was given in the lesson in Chapter 5.

4. Wheel of Life Activity

Complete the wheel of life exercise which you can find below. Answer as many of the questions as you like and think about and identify an area where you would like to increase your satisfaction.

https://wheeloflife.noomii.com/

How did this affect what you want to work on and what you can do in this challenge?

5. Three Good Things Activity

Write down three good things that happen during the next day and think of how you might continue to use an exercise like this to continue to see and create more good things in your life.

1. ____

____

2. ____

____

3. ____

____

How can you continue to use an exercise like this to see and create more good things in your life?

____

____

____

____

____

____

____

____

Part 2 – Bringing Out Your Best

What is this part about?

Purpose: The purpose of this part is to enable you to better see, appreciate, and use what is best in yourself to increase your happiness, well-being, success, and make the most of your life.

Topics: There are chapters about discovering your best, the value of being true to yourself, and on how to increase the perseverance, courage, self-efficacy or belief in yourself, and self-control you will need to be successful.

Activities: The most important activities focus on identifying your strengths, using them in new ways, and better understanding how to use them to achieve the goals that will enable you to create and realize the kind of life that you want most for yourself.

Chapter 7

Discovering Your Best

Do the best you can until you know better.
Then when you know better, do better.
— Maya Angelou

Welcome to the second part of the positive psychology challenge! The first part was basic training for making the most of your life and living your life to the fullest. You had an introduction to positive psychology, learned about happiness, and the theory of PERMA about the five elements of well-being. You also learned about three things that you will help you increase them: (1) positive reappraisal which is the ability change your mind for the better, (2) behavioral activation which involves finding and doing what you love to do, and (3) exposure to what you fear as a way of increasing your courage for overcoming obstacles. The three good things activity included in almost all of the chapters was a way of opening your eyes to more of the goodness and beauty around you every day.

During this second part of the challenge, we will focus on enabling you to better see and use what is best about yourself. During the next third part, we will concentrate on improving your relationships with others and the world around you before focusing on helping you create a plan for a better future in the fourth and final part.

As I said in the first chapter, before the dawn of the positive psychology movement, the focus in psychology was primarily on what can go wrong with us. Psychology and psychiatry developed what is called the Diagnostic and Statistical Manual or DSM. This was developed to classify all of the mental and behavioral problems that may affect us, including things like anxiety, depression, ADHD, substance abuse, bipolar disorder, eating disorders, schizophrenia, and PTSD.

To balance what can go wrong with what can go right, Martin Seligman and Chris Peterson led the development of what has been jokingly called the "UN-DSM," a manual that classifies the attitudes, behaviors, and strengths that enable us to be happy, successful, and create a life worth living. They recruited a large, diverse, and well-respected group of psychologists and social scientists from around the world. This group met frequently during the early years of positive psychology and came up with a new classification of human virtues and strengths. Their goal was to identify the things that across time and culture represent us at our best and contribute to both individual and community happiness and well-being.

The result is what is called the Values in Actions or VIA classification of virtues and strengths. It is presented in that "UN-DSM" or what is more formally titled the *Character*

Strengths and Virtues: A Handbook and Classification. They also developed a survey that you are asked to take for this chapter that will enable you to identify your top strengths. Most important, during the past 20 years, they and other positive psychologists have identified and developed a growing number of ways to build and use each of the strengths. Unlike the fictional powers in *Star Wars* or *Harry Potter*, these strengths represent the real powers that are within our grasp and that can help us create the kind of lives we seek.

Thus, we are focusing on many of these strengths in different chapters in this challenge and in this part will help you identify and learn how to better use your top strengths on your journey. To begin, I want to introduce the 24 strengths as they are classified under six overarching virtues. As I go through these, see if you can identify some that you think may be top strengths for you:

The first virtue is Wisdom, which enables us to find our way in life, and it includes the strengths of Wisdom itself; Curiosity; Love of Learning; Open-mindedness; and Creativity.

The second virtue is Courage, which enables us to overcome obstacles to moving forward in our lives, and it includes the strengths of Bravery; Authenticity, Honesty, and Integrity; Perseverance; and Vitality or Zest.

The third virtue is Humanity, which enables us to establish and maintain good relationships with other people and it includes the strengths of Love; Kindness; and Social or Emotional Intelligence.

The fourth virtue is Justice, which enables us to create a healthy and just society and includes Fairness; Citizenship or Teamwork; and Leadership.

The fifth virtue is Temperance, which helps us keep balance in our lives, and it includes Self Control; Humility; Forgiveness; and Prudence – which has to do with careful planning.

The sixth and final virtue is Transcendence, which enable us to connect with things larger than ourselves, and it includes Optimism and Hope; Appreciation of Beauty and Excellence; Gratitude; Humor and Playfulness; and Meaning, Purpose, and Spirituality.

Now that you know what these virtues and strengths are, I need to make a critical point about them. Because of our negativity bias and tendency to focus so much on our disorders; many people primarily focus on correcting their weaknesses - the strengths that that are lower - rather than how to better use their top strengths.

The difference between working on your weaknesses and finding new ways to use your strengths has been compared to a sailboat that represents each of us. Working on our weaknesses is like fixing the holes in the boat. Sometimes it is necessary but usually not a lot of fun and if it is all we do we may never really get anywhere. In contrast, focusing on better using our top strengths - like you will do in this part of the challenge - is like lifting the sails! When we do that, we really begin to get somewhere and it will feel like having the wind at our backs.

This is like finding things you love to do, "following your bliss" in Joseph Campbell's terms, or experiencing flow - which often involves the expression of our top strengths. The other thing is that once you experience that wind at your back in using your strengths, it is often not as hard to work on the holes in your boat - and using your top strengths can help with that. In this challenge, you will get good ideas for building the strengths that you struggle with, but the most important thing is that you begin to realize that you already have sails and that you begin to lift them and see what happens!

You can see the power of this in the life of the singer-songwriter Stevie Wonder, who was blind as a young child, although he had an exquisite sense of hearing. The turning point in his young life came when a mouse got loose in his elementary school classroom one day. After the class tried to find it without success, the teacher remembered little Stevie's gift for hearing and asked him to use it to find the mouse.

The whole class got quiet and Stevie began to hear what others couldn't. He followed the sound to the wastebasket where the mouse was hiding. The class cheered and thereafter Stevie began to see himself more in terms of his strengths rather than his weaknesses. This led him to embrace his gift for hearing and become one of the most creative and successful musicians of the past 40-50 years. During that day in class, he felt the wind at his back, and I hope you will begin to feel that same wind during this part of our challenge – which brings us to the tasks for this lesson.

Workbook Tasks for the Chapter

These tasks are designed to help you better identify your top strengths, reflect on when you have used them, and recognize strengths in other people.

First, as after every chapter, there is a link to a video where you can see and hear me going over the lesson for this chapter.

Second, there is a task that involves going to the website where you can take the Values in Action (VIA) Survey that will enable you to identify your top strengths. After you complete the survey, you will be given a ranking of the 24 VIA strengths from your highest to lowest. This will be an important first step in seeing, embracing, and using what is best in yourself and for the activities that will involve using your top strengths during the rest of this part of the challenge. Although you may see options for paying for a larger report on the VIA Survey website, all you need for completing the tasks in this workbook is the ranking of your 24 strengths which doesn't cost anything.

Third, there is an activity where you will be asked to list your top five strengths from the VIA Survey and write about a time you were at your best using at least one of your top strengths. Just as it can be very helpful to think and write about times you have been resilient or benefited from stress, so it can be very useful to remember and reflect on the times you have used your top strengths. This can improve your confidence and motivation to use them and make it more likely you will benefit from using them in the future.

Fourth, there is a task for beginning to practice what has been called "strength spotting," which will improve your ability to see and empower the best in others. Below, there is a list of the 24 VIA strengths with a brief description of each and a link to a special video of a scene from the movie *Good Will Hunting*. The task for you will be to circle the strengths that you see in either the Robin Williams or the Matt Damon character.

Fifth, there also is a copy of the list of 24 VIA strengths in Appendix G. The final task is for you to use it to identify the strengths in one of your friends or family members. If you can, share your list with them and try to let them know when, where, and how you have seen the strengths that you identified in them. Then you can ask them to identify your strengths and you can talk about how to better support each other in using your strengths. This is one of the best ways to increase your ability to see the best in other people.

1. Author's Video for this Chapter

Here is the link for the video of me going over the lesson for this chapter.

https://youtu.be/PCxzb3G_eiE

2. Take the VIA Survey Activity

This task involves going to the following link where you can take the VIA Survey which will give you a ranking from the highest to the lowest on each of the 24 strengths. There are options for paying for longer reports but all you need to do is get your ranking of the 24 strengths, which is free.

https://www.viacharacter.org/survey/account/register

3. Using Your Strengths While at Your Best

What are your top five strengths according to the VIA Survey that you took?

1. ______________________________

2. ______________________________

3. ______________________________

4. ______________________________

5. ______________________________

What is a time you were at your best using at least one of your top five strengths?

____

____

____

____

____

____

____

____

____

____

4. Strength Spotting in a Movie

Watch the video clip below from the movie "Good Will Hunting" and use the Strength Spotting sheet below to check off the strengths that you see in the counselor character played by Robin Williams and his patient played by Matt Damon.

"Good Will Hunting – Park scene subtitled":

https://www.youtube.com/watch?v=8GY-iWnriGg

Below is a list and brief description of the 24 VIA strengths in their six categories. Which of these do you see in the counselor character (played by Robin Williams) and the patient character (played by Matt Damon)? When you see a strength use the initial C for the counselor and P for patient. If you find that they both display the same strength, then mark both initials.

WISDOM

_____ **Creativity:** ingenuity; sees & does things in new/unique ways; original and adaptive ideas

_____ **Curiosity:** novelty-seeker; takes an interest; open to different experiences; asks questions

_____ **Open-mindedness & Judgment:** critical thinker; analytical; logical; thinks things through

_____ **Love of learning:** masters new skills & topics; passionate about knowledge & learning
_____ **Wisdom:** wise; provides wise counsel; sees the big pictures; integrates others' views.

COURAGE

_____ **Bravery:** valorous; does not shrink from fear; speaks up for what's right
_____ **Perseverance:** persistent; industrious; overcomes obstacles; finishes what is started
_____ **Authenticity, Integrity, & Honesty**: genuine, true to one's values; truthful
_____ **Zest:** enthusiastic; energetic; vital; feels alive and activated

HUMANITY

_____ **Love:** gives and accepts love; values close relations with others
_____ **Kindness:** generous; nurturing; caring; compassionate; altruistic
_____ **Social and/or Emotional Intelligence:** aware of the motives and feelings of oneself & others, know what makes other people tick

JUSTICE

_____ **Citizenship and/or Teamwork:** a team player; community-focused; socially responsible; loyal
_____ **Fairness:** acts upon principles of justice; does not allow feelings to bias decisions about others
_____ **Leadership**: organizes group activities; encourages and leads groups to get things done

TEMPERANCE

_____ **Forgiveness:** merciful; accepts others' shortcomings; gives people a second chance
_____ **Humility:** modest; lets accomplishments speak for themselves; focuses on others
_____ **Prudence:** careful; wisely cautious; thinks before speaking; does not take undue risks
_____ **Self-control:** self-controlled; disciplined; manages impulses & emotions

TRANSCENDENCE

_____ **Appreciation of Beauty & Excellence:** awe-filled; quickly moved to wonder; marvels at beauty & greatness
_____ **Gratitude:** thanks for the good; expresses thanks; feels blessed
_____ **Optimism & Hope:** optimistic; future-minded; has a positive outlook
_____ **Humor:** playful; enjoys joking and bringing smiles to others; lighthearted
_____ **Meaning, Purpose, & Spirituality:** meaning and purpose-driven, religious and/or spiritual

5. Strength Spotting in a Relationship

The final task involves using a copy of the Strength Spotting sheet in Appendix G that is like the once you used in the previous task involving spotting strengths in a movie. There are two parts to this task.

The first part is to use Strength Spotting Sheet to identify the strengths of one of your friends or family members. If you can, share your list with them and let them know when, where, and how you have seen the strengths that you identified in them.

What strengths did you highlight in the other person and what was it like to talk with them about their strengths?

The second part of this task is to give a copy of the Strength Spotting sheet to the person whose strengths you tried to identify and ask them to use it to identify your strengths. Once you have done this for each other, then you can begin to talk about how you can work together to help each other better use your top strengths.

What strengths did they highlight and what was it like to talk with them about your strengths? How can you encourage and support each other in better using your strengths?

Chapter 8

Authenticity

Be who you are and say what you feel,
because those who mind don't matter
and those who matter don't mind.
— Bernard Baruch

I hope that taking the VIA Survey helped you begin to discover more about your strengths. It is one of the best tools we have for discovering more of what is best in ourselves. I would also encourage you to let more of your friends and family members know about it and ask them to take it so that you can share your results. As with one of the tasks at the end of the last chapter, you can also copy the Strength Spotting sheet in Appendix G and use it to spot and point out the strengths that you see in each other.

This brings us to our lesson for this chapter, which is about authenticity and the importance of being true to ourselves. It includes being true to our strengths and our weaknesses, our talents, gifts, and interests, and all that makes up who we are – even when those around us may not be able to recognize, acknowledge, or accept it.

There are few words that express what positive psychology has to offer regarding authenticity better than the simple words of Cyndi Lauper in the song *True Colors*:

"You with the sad eyes
Don't be discouraged
Oh, I realize
It's hard to take courage
In a world full of people
You can lose sight of it all
And the darkness inside you
Can make you feel so small.

But I see your true colors
Shining through
I see your true colors
And that's why I love you
So, don't be afraid to let them show
Your true colors
True colors are beautiful
Like a rainbow."

You know that psychologists and people in the academic world can get lost in using big words to get published and tenure - and to get other people to accept and admire them. But look at that first verse.

There are a lot of those sad eyes in psychologists who only pay attention to abnormal or clinical psychology. In addition, there are many others who get overwhelmed with our bias towards the negative, what is worst in the world, in other people, or in themselves. The first verse says, "You can lose sight of it all, and the darkness inside you can make you feel so small."

That survey you took; those words used to describe those strengths; we work hard to develop vaccinations from out of control viruses, but we miss the psychological vaccine that might keep us from being overwhelmed by that inner darkness. The words for those strengths, those good things about us, and the ability to see and name them; they may be just the vaccine that the doctor ordered!

Cyndi Lauper is singing about what psychologists like Carl Rogers, Abraham Maslow, and Carol Ryff had already been focusing on and what has come to the center for positive psychologists like Martin Seligman, Chris Peterson, and Barbara Fredrickson.

Take a look at the second verse. Positive psychology has given us the words and the vision to see the full truth about ourselves – not just our weaknesses and disorders – but now also the remarkable attitudes, behaviors, and strengths that enable us to be at our best.

"I see your true colors and that's why I love you."

That's why I love you? If we can't see ourselves in the light of love - then of course we may get lost in anxiety, depression, and stress. Carl Rogers thought that if you grow up surrounded by those who love and accept you for who you are - that you will very likely become someone who can do the same for others and will want to give back to the world. Research has found that troubled children and adolescents who have just one person they trust and who believes in them can make all the difference in enabling them to be resilient and learn and grow from the stress that they experience.

Not only that, but isn't it a natural human response to love someone when they put themselves out there and really make themselves vulnerable to us? In the special video for this chapter, you will see the social work researcher Brené Brown talk about this. She has done studies showing that taking the risk of being vulnerable with others may be a critical part of building and sustaining the kind of relationships that we all need in order to be happy and feel like we belong.

When we see someone reaching out in a vulnerable way to us, we often feel that they are taking a risk to give us a gift and we might feel like saying the words in the song: "that's why I love you." We might add the words, "I can see you, I can see myself in you, and I can see us reaching our destination – in the joy and sense of fulfillment of being true to who we are." But the message of Brené Brown, the healing power of taking a risk in reaching out to others, and much of positive psychology may be even better than the second verse.

This second verse says, "don't be afraid to let them show." People like Brené and those in positive psychology would say, "Okay, so it is natural to be afraid, you are not alone, and the fear that you are feeling doesn't have to stop you." They might also add, "I see you and I got you!" "I see your true colors shining through!"

Next, in the song there are words that you will probably never find in the Diagnostic and Statistical Manual of Mental Disorders or in the report of a clinical psychologist, "You are beautiful – like a rainbow!" The "rain of that darkness that makes us feel so small," is transformed by those colors shining through in being true to ourselves – and then suddenly we don't feel small!

But I'm not just saying this because Cyndi, Carl, and Brené said it. I've definitely seen this hypothesis tested and supported after many years of trying to be true to the good, the bad, and the ugly in myself. However, the best evidence I've seen is in what happens with the students in a small advanced positive psychology lab class that I've taught more than a dozen times. In this class, the students have a simple assignment that is great for them, because they don't have to hear me talk more, and great for me, because I don't really have to do anything except take it all in.

The assignment is to simply have each student give examples of when they have used their top strengths, in front of the class of 20-25 students. The rest of the class each have one of those Strength Spotting sheets and check what they see and then write whatever they can about whatever goodness and beauty they see in the speaker. What happens? Well, it never fails and makes me want to sing that song! With amazing consistency and infinite variety, the students talk about how they used what is best in themselves to do often incredibly difficult and inspiring things like overcoming abuse, bullying, and rejection. Moreover, they end up shining brighter than the rainbow in that song.

And what has happened without fail is that by the end of the semester, there is a community – maybe the kind that most people never get to experience – where people see and bring out the best in each other in spite of the worst that has happened to them. Together they move from surviving to thriving as they witness how to make it happen in the lives and stories of their fellow students and people just like them.

So, in coming to the close of this lesson, the good news from positive psychology about authenticity is twofold. First, that being true to ourselves is critically important for our survival and for thriving and flourishing – and that sometimes we need to take a risk in putting ourselves out there.

Second, that our ability to be authentic goes hand-in-hand with just the kind of community that we hope this challenge will make more possible for you to discover and create. In order to be true and love and accept ourselves for who we are, we need to seek out and create the kind of community that welcomes it. There will be much more about this in the third part of this challenge, where you will learn about what we can do to improve our relationships and community - which we know are a primary source of our happiness and well-being.

But for now, those colors, those strengths - don't be afraid to let them show! On this journey you are not alone. Even if you are afraid, watch the Brené Brown video and begin taking little risks with those you trust and then see what happens.

Workbook Tasks for the Chapter

The tasks for this chapter involve finding new ways to use your top strengths, the value of being vulnerable with other people, and understanding value of authenticity.

First, as after every chapter, there is a link to a video where you can see and hear me going over the lesson for this chapter.

Second, there is a task that involves going online to find a list of different ways you can use the VIA strengths, reading the sections about the top five strengths that were identified for you on the VIA Survey, and then thinking about and writing down new ways that you can use each of these strengths.

Third, the next activity builds on the last. It involves using two of your top five strengths in a new way in the next week or two. This is the primary kind of task that you will build on during this part of the challenge. Research has shown that it has consistently been an effective way for us to increase our happiness and well-being.

Fourth, these is a special video of a TED talk for you to watch called "The Power of Vulnerability" by Brené Brown. This has been one of the most watched TED talks of all time and one that many former students have found to be very powerful in bringing about positive changes in their lives. After you watch it, there are questions that ask you to think about when you may have taken a risk in being vulnerable in the way she talks about.

Fifth, there are reflection questions asking you to write about a time when you were true to yourself in the past and also when you might want to be more true to yourself in the future. Writing about when you have been true to yourself is a way of building courage and confidence for doing it more in the future. Writing about when you might want to be true to yourself in the future can be a way of exposing yourself to what you are afraid of, like we talked about in Chapter 3, so that your anxiety and fear will become reduced while your courage for being vulnerable grows.

1. Author's Video for this Chapter

Here is the link for the video of me going over the lesson for this chapter.

https://youtu.be/iTvmXXRKJLY

2. Planning New Ways to Use Your Strengths

Read the sections of the "340 Ways to Use Character Strengths" by Tayyab Rashid about your top five strengths and write down three new ways you can use each of those five strengths.

You can find it here: http://tayyabrashid.com/pdf/via_strengths.pdf

My Strength #1 is: ______________________________ New ways I can use it are:

1. ____

2. ____

3. ____

My Strength #2 is: ______________________________ New ways I can use it are:

1. ____

2. ____

3. ____

My Strength #3 is: ______________________________ New ways I can use it are:

1. ____

2. ____

3. ____

My Strength #4 is: ______________________________ New ways I can use it are:

1. ____

2. ____

3. ____

My Strength #5 is: ______________________________ New ways I can use it are:

1. ____

2. ____

3. ____

3. Using Your Strengths in New Ways

Use two of your top strengths in one of the new ways that you identified in the next week or two. What strength did you use and how? How did you feel in using them? What happened when you used them?

4. Special Video - "The Power of Vulnerability | Brené Brown"

https://www.youtube.com/watch?v=iCvmsMzlF7o

After you watch the video, reflect on and write about a time when you were vulnerable in the way that Brené Brown talks about.

How were you vulnerable? What do you think enabled you to be vulnerable and what happened when you were?

5. Reflection Questions

What was a time you were true to yourself in the past? What do think helped you to do it?

When would you like to be more true to yourself in the future? What do you think would help you do it?

Chapter 9

Perseverance

The journey of a thousand miles begins with a single step.
— Lao Tzu

So far in the second part of this challenge, you have identified your strengths and learned about the value of being true to yourself. In this chapter and the next, we are going to talk about two other things that might be necessary for moving forward in being true to the best of ourselves – especially in the face of stress and whatever obstacles we may face.

In this chapter, we will be focusing on one of the simple strengths that we are exercising every time we decide not to give up. In the next chapter, we will focus on courage itself – although it will not just be physical courage but also other forms of courage we may need much more often.

This first simple strength that we are going to talk about in this chapter is perseverance, and we are also going to talk about two of its close cousins, who I think you will really enjoy meeting!

But first, I want to let you know about a few people you may have heard of who had to persevere after they failed, fell down, or were defeated.

When he was a young man, Walt Disney was fired from a newspaper because his boss thought he lacked imagination and had no original ideas.

Before they hit it big, the Beatles were turned down by the Decca recording company by an executive who said, "We don't like their sound and guitar music is on the way out."

Before she became rich and famous and beloved around the world, Oprah Winfrey was told that she was fired from her job as a news anchor because she "wasn't fit for television."

Before becoming what many people think is the greatest basketball player of all time, after he was cut from his high school basketball team, Michael Jordan went home, locked himself in his room, and cried.

Before becoming famous for writing the *Harry Potter* books and making more than a billion dollars, J.W. Rowling was a struggling single mother on welfare whose book was rejected 12 times.

This next person is probably the closest to a legend that the United States has ever had. But before he became what many think is the best president in U.S. history, Abraham Lincoln's fiancé died, he failed in business twice, had a nervous breakdown, and was defeated in eight elections.

The final person that I want to mention did not speak until he was four years old, did not read until he was seven; causing his teachers to think he was mentally handicapped, slow, and anti-social. Albert Einstein eventually won the Nobel Prize and changed the face of modern physics!

These are prime examples of the power of perseverance or simply refusing to give up. This power is often expressed in a simple saying that probably has a version in nearly all languages and cultures around the world, "The longest journey begins with a simple step." As you think about what you want in your life, perseverance is a great equalizer that makes it possible for even the smallest, weakest, and most flawed among us to have a chance.

Why is this simple strength so powerful and so important for our happiness and success? Fortunately, there have been enough research psychologists who didn't give up until they got some answers!

First, perseverance makes it more likely to attain difficult goals. That is, perseverance is generally rewarded with success - maybe not every time, but it usually is eventually, and that is the point.

Second, perseverance enhances our enjoyment of success. If we make it the first time without having to really try, then reaching that goal may not mean as much to us.

Third, perseverance can also have benefits that have nothing to do with our original goals. Going out for the Tee-ball team until we make it as a child won't translate into an adult career in Tee-ball, but it may teach us an incredibly important lesson about persevering in other ways that will help us succeed as an adult.

Fourth and last, perseverance can increase our sense of self-efficacy – which is the belief that we can do what it takes to reach one of our goals.

So, this is perseverance and why it is so important. But I also mentioned two of its close cousins and how much I thought you might also like to meet them. You will hear more about the first of these cousins in the special video for this chapter. The word for it has been in the title of a couple famous western movies as well as what we sometimes call something that becomes stuck between our teeth. The word is "grit" and its meaning here is perseverance – plus!

This kind of grit has been studied by Angela Duckworth who has shown it to often be more important for success than things like IQ or physical strength. It turns out that grit may also be something that is a lot easier for us to increase. I said that grit is perseverance plus, and I literally meant it. The two parts of grit are, one, perseverance and, two, having a long-term goal or purpose that you maintain and continue to be passionate about. The idea is that when you put them together, they produce more beautiful music than just John Lennon or Paul McCartney alone.

So, perseverance alone is very good, but if you can combine it with the kind of authentic passion or purpose we have been talking about – watch out! Out of those things that you love to do, try to find the ones that you love the most. Out of those ways that you can experience flow, see if you can organize them around a long-term goal that is true to who you are and what you want most. If you do these things and use your strengths to "follow your bliss," like Joseph Campbell talks about – well, that is where you get a Michael Jordan, Oprah, J.K. Rowling, Honest Ab, or the best of who you can be!

The other encouraging but also challenging cousin of perseverance is called "growth mindset" – which has been contrasted with what psychologist Carol Dweck calls "fixed mindset." While both of these mindsets are related to how successful we are, they really come into play when we fail. When you fail a test, are rejected, lose a job, or don't make the team – the temptation is to adopt a fixed mindset that says the reason you didn't reach your goal was because of something inherent about you that you can't change.

In contrast, that "growth mindset" cousin was raised on generous helpings of positive reappraisal and the possibility of stress-related growth. Growth mindset is the perspective that rather than being a final statement on the inherent limitations of who you are and what you can do, a failure or set-back is actually an opportunity to learn so that you can do better next time and eventually be successful. Combine this with that long-term passion and purpose thing that Angela Duckworth talks about, and you are really on your way!

So, however you ranked on perseverance in the VIA Survey, you really have no excuse, and you should invite the cousins over. Perseverance means simply taking another one of those single steps, grit adds a purpose that we are passionate about and asks if this is something we really want, and growth mindset says, "Okay, I am going to perform a Jedi mind trick when the inevitable happens. When I fail, I am going to use it as the occasion to learn what I need for getting it right next time!"

So, first be clear about what you really want. That is why we began by trying to help you identify that in the first part of this challenge. Once you get a good idea of what would genuinely make you happy and the strengths you can use to make it happen – that is where perseverance comes in to enable you to bring it all home. The good news is that if you just keep at it, you are much more likely to eventually get there.

Finally, growth mindset may bring us a more powerful message than the often quoted words of Friedrich Nietzsche who said, "What doesn't kill me, makes me stronger." Growth mindset says that what doesn't kill me, even if I fail in the process, may not only make me stronger but also wiser and probably a lot happier!

Workbook Tasks for the Chapter

The tasks for this chapter will help you better understand the value of grit, use your strengths to experience flow and increase your happiness, and learn about when and how to best exercise perseverance.

First, as after every chapter, there is a link to a video where you can see and hear me going over the lesson for this chapter.

Second, there is a video about that cousin "grit" that we talked about. It is a TED talk by Angela Duckworth who first began to study grit and show how important it can be. She was a student of Martin Seligman, the primary founder of positive psychology. This video will help you better understand why grit may be so important in helping you reach your goals.

Third, there is an activity that involves using one of your top strengths to put yourself in the experience of flow. We may often be using our top strengths when we are in flow and this activity may help you find new ways to experience flow. It may also help you see how beneficial it can be for success and living our lives to the fullest. If you remember the sailboat metaphor that was introduced in Chapter 7, the experience of flow is often like having the wind at our backs when we lift the sails in using our top strengths.

Fourth, there a writing activity that asks you to list three of your top strengths that you think may most enable you to increase your happiness and well-being in the future. This will increase your motivation to use your strengths and help you get a better idea of how and when to best use them.

Finally, there are reflection questions about when it might be most important for you to persevere, when it might be best not to persevere, and what might help you best know how to decide between the two. Of course, this is related to *The Serenity Prayer* written by the theologian Reinhold Niebuhr:

"God, grant me the serenity to accept the things I cannot change,
courage to change the things I can,
and wisdom to know the difference."

Like all of the VIA strengths, just as we may sometimes not use them enough, there are others times when we may use them too much. Perseverance is one of those strengths where the wisdom to know the difference between when to keep going and when to stop may be especially important.

1. Author's Video for this Lesson

Here is the link for the video of me going over the lesson for this chapter.

https://youtu.be/v_UuF1g1jP8

2. Special Video - "Grit: the power of passion and perseverance | Angela Lee Duckworth"

After you watch the video, reflect on when you have used grit and when it may be most beneficial for you to use it in the future.

https://www.youtube.com/watch?v=H14bBuluwB8

3. Use a Top Strength to Put Yourself in Flow

Use one of your top strengths in a way that may put you into the experience of flow that was described in Chapter 2, when we covered the element of Engagement in Martin

Seligman's PERMA theory of well-being. Try to do something that might put you into a flow state in a new and different way than what you may have experienced in the past.

If you need help coming up with ideas, you can review the 340 Ways to Use Character Strengths that we gave you the link for at the end of Chapter 8. You can also 'google' it by entering the title. It might also be useful for you to review the Pleasant Activities List in Appendix F for ideas of different things that you might want to do. After you have tried to use one of your top strengths to experience flow, then answer the questions below.

What strength did you try to use and how did you use it to try to experience flow? What happened when you did it? What did you learn from the experience?

____

____

____

____

____

____

____

____

____

____

4. Using Your Top Strengths to be Happy

List three of your top strengths that you think may do the most to increase your happiness and well-being and write about how you can best use each strength to make this happen.

1. The first top strength for increasing my happiness and well-being is:

____

How I can use this strength to increase my happiness and well-being:

____

____

____

____

____

2. The second top strength for increasing my happiness and well-being is:

____

How I can use this strength to increase my happiness and well-being:

____

____

____

____

____

____

3. The third top strength for increasing my happiness and well-being is:

____

How I can use this strength to increase my happiness and well-being:

5. Reflection Questions

What are the situations and circumstances in your life when you think it may be important for you to persevere and not give up?

What are the situations and circumstances in your life when you think it might be important not to continue to persevere?

What might help you best decide when to persevere and when to stop trying?

Chapter 10

Courage

The only thing to fear is fear itself.
— Franklin Delano Roosevelt

You are now halfway through the second part this challenge. The first part was basic training. The second part is focused on discovering and using your strengths and what is best in you to make the most of your life. During the first part, you learned about how to foster a classic human virtue and strength that can show us the way and enable us to make tough decisions: wisdom. In this chapter, you will learn about an equally classic human virtue and strength that can give us the emotional "oomph" we need to move forward despite obstacles and fear: courage!

We may not often see the relationship between wisdom and courage and how much courage may depend on wisdom. But it is wisdom that can prevent courage from falling into doing something that is rash, stupid, or just plain dumb. What is courage? Its root is in the Latin and Greek words for "heart."

Earl Shelp has defined courage as having three components:

1. There is a significant risk of harm or loss.
2. There is a judgment – and this is where wisdom comes in – that the potential benefits of an action may outweigh the risks.
3. There is both the willingness and the ability to carry out the action.

There is one very important thing that is missing from this definition – and this one thing may broaden the occasions and possibilities of courage for us all. Did you catch it? This definition does not say that courage means that we are not afraid. In fact, when there is significant risk of harm or loss, there may be something wrong with us if we don't at least feel a little fear.

Now here is where courage comes home to matter tremendously for each of us. When I say the word bravery or courage, what do you think of? If you are like most people, you may think of a soldier putting him or herself at risk in battle or a firefighter going in to save someone in a burning building. These are examples of physical courage – which we may indeed be challenged to show at some points in our lives.

But one of the breakthroughs in the positive psychological study of courage has been to extend it to include the kinds of courage we are much more likely to need in our everyday lives. There are at least two other kinds of courage that, in addition to physical courage, may be critical for making the most of our lives, on the one hand, and for building a community that makes this possible for all of us, on the other.

The first kind has been called "personal courage" and the second has been called "moral courage." Personal courage is the kind of courage we are asking you to display the most in this challenge. It is what will enable you to answer the call to adventure in entering a new and unknown place in your life. Sometimes we will do almost anything to avoid the unknown, including staying in an abusive relationship or toxic work environment, continuing with an addiction, or not asking for help when we really need it.

Personal courage is the willingness and ability to take a calculated risk – even when we are anxious or afraid – in doing something that may help us really move forward in our lives. It is what you have already been doing in this challenge if you have gotten this far. You have dared to try something new that may change you and how you see the world. You have dared to pay attention to something other than just the holes in your sailboat. You have begun to see and lift the sails. It takes personal courage to do that and see where it takes you. So, whether or not you can relate to the physical courage of a soldier or those firefighters during September 11, we can all relate to the personal courage it takes to leave our comfort zone and take the risks necessary for creating a life that is worth living.

But in addition to physical and personal courage, there is another kind of courage that is so easy to miss, especially in the world of psychology that focuses so much on the individual and not the larger community and world. It turns out that human beings are inherently social animals and that a necessary part of our happiness is intimately tied to that of those around us.

This calls for moral courage, which is taking calculated risks for other people and the larger community. It is the willingness and ability to speak up and do the right thing in the face of negative consequences, such as the loss of income, relationships, jobs, social status, and the approval of others. Examples of moral courage include Rosa Parks risking being arrested and going to jail for not sitting in the back of the bus and Mahatma Gandhi refusing to eat until the Hindus and Muslins in India stopped fighting.

While moral courage may result in some unwanted consequences to us as individuals, it also means gaining something that no one can take away from us – the satisfaction of knowing that we did the right thing. I once asked my students to rate their willingness to try each of the 340 Ways to Use Strengths that you were asked to review in Chapter 8. Several of the top rated were examples of moral courage like standing up for those who can't stand up for themselves and resisting peer pressure in speaking out against an injustice.

Thus, while we may sometimes hear the call to display physical courage – we may more frequently hear it for personal and moral courage.

There is one other thing that is important to say about courage. Robert Biswas-Diener has written about what he calls "the courage quotient." He defines courage in mathematical terms by saying that whether we will act in a courageous way depends on our willingness to act divided by the fear we are feeling about acting. He thinks that the two things we can do to increase courage are (1) to decrease our fear and (2) to increase our willingness and motivation for acting.

We have already begun planting the seeds for doing both in the challenge. First, we can decrease our fear by gradually exposing ourselves to what we are afraid of with the support of others. We can do something like mindful breathing to relax and calm ourselves so we can see and think more clearly.

Second, we can increase our willingness and motivation to act by focusing on the satisfaction, gratification, and likely reward of our courageous action and by creatively using positive reappraisal to help us see a better path to it.

A simple example from my life was when I first fell in love as a teenager. I was terrified to talk to girls. But I was so enamored with this particular girl that despite my abject fear, I was actually able to call her and ask her for date. I finally had a motivation that was stronger than my fear. But the reward may not just be in getting the girl or the boy, but even more in the confidence that you can do the courageous thing when it is called for.

So, the lesson for this chapter has been about courage, which is essential for this challenge and for a life worth living. As you begin to realize how much more you are capable of in using your strengths, you will see abundant opportunities for practicing courage. Once you decide to do something that requires courage, you can use what you have learned to reduce your fear and increase your motivation by focusing on the potential benefits of acting courageously.

Workbook Tasks for the Chapter

The tasks for this chapter will help you understand and see the value of courage in your life and how you can use your top strengths to have a positive impact on other people in your life.

First, as after every chapter, there is a link to a video where you can see and hear me going over the lesson for this chapter.

Second, there is a link for a special video that shows an extraordinary example of personal and moral courage in the life of a 6-year-old girl. This has been another video that I could often see strong reactions in the students in class when they have watched it. It is a wonderful example of how children can sometimes show the wisdom and the courage that adults may sometimes lack.

Third, the next task involves writing about a time when you showed courage and what may have enabled you to be courageous. Just be sure to look for times you may have shown personal or moral courage as well as times you may have expressed physical courage. Also, just as a good way to boost resilience or the use of your top strengths is to remember a when were you successful in the past, so too thinking and writing about when you were courageous in the past can be a great way of increasing your confidence and the likelihood of being that way in the future.

Fourth, there are reflection questions about where and when you would most like to display courage in the future and what might help you to act courageously when the time comes. Just imagining and rehearsing a situation in the future where you may need courage can reduce the fear and anxiety you will feel at the time.

Finally, once again there is a task that involves using one of your top strengths in a new way, but this time you are asked to do it with the goal of having a positive impact on someone else. While it may be beneficial to use your top strengths in a new way even without a specific goal in mind, it may be may be that much better for other people and for you to use it to express love and kindness. You will learn much more about the benefits of these two strengths when we focus on them in the third part of the challenge.

1. Author's Video for this Lesson

Here is the link for the video of me going over the lesson for this chapter.

https://youtu.be/2gOSNDKB3CM

2. Special Video – "Adorable Girl Tells her Divorced Parents to be Friends"

Watch the video and think about when it might be beneficial for you to try to show similar courage in speaking out to someone who is in authority or has some kind of power over you.

https://www.youtube.com/watch?v=DCNUlEfD_dg

3. When You Showed Courage

What was a time when you were courageous and what enabled you to be that way?

____

____

____

____

____

____

____

4. Reflection Questions:

When and where would you most like to display courage in the future? What might help you act in a courageous way?

5. Using a Top Strength in a New Way to Positively Impact Others

This activity involves thinking about how you can use your top strengths to benefit others and then doing something to use one of these strengths in this way and seeing what happens. The first step is to brainstorm about what you may be able to do and the second step is to choose one thing to do and see what happens when you try it.

What are some ways that you can use your top strengths to benefit someone who is important to you?

____

____

____

____

____

____

____

How did you use one of your top strengths to benefit someone important to you? How did you feel when you were doing it and how do you think it affected you both?

____

____

____

____

____

____

____

Chapter 11

Self-Efficacy

My father gave me the greatest gift
anyone could give another person,
he believed in me.

— Jim Valvano

In the last two chapters, we have talked about two basic human strengths that make it possible for us to overcome the obstacles that may get in our way. The focus of this chapter has a name that may not be very familiar to those outside of psychology. At the same time, it is hard to imagine anything that is more relevant to everything we do or that has been embraced more broadly around the world.

Self-efficacy is its name and this name was coined by the psychologist Albert Bandura who first studied it. Self-efficacy is easy to confuse with self-esteem and what we will be talking about in the next chapter – self-control. Whereas self-esteem has to do with how favorably we view ourselves, self-efficacy has a more particular focus and is defined as "your belief in your ability to do what it takes to reach a specific goal."

There are two things to make clear about self-efficacy. First, self-efficacy doesn't have to do with your actual ability to do something, only your belief about whether you can do it. Second, self-efficacy is usually associated with a specific goal or activity, such as being able to pass a math class, stick to a schedule, or run a marathon; rather than about being able to do anything and everything.

Let me try to make the first point clear with an example. Let's say that the basketball player LeBron James had a twin brother who was his equal in terms of height, speed, agility, intelligence, and the ability to dunk. Let's say that they were on two basketball teams that were equal in every way and that they met in the NBA championship.

The only difference between LeBron #1 and LeBron #2 is that Lebron #1 has a stronger belief in his ability to play basketball than his brother LeBron #2. Even though the twin LeBron's are equal in ability, experience, and everything else, the research on self-efficacy strongly suggests that LeBron #1 will play better and that his team will be more likely to win the championship.

This is the power of self-efficacy - the power of believing that you can do what it takes to reach a goal. Self-efficacy is one of the most powerful and useful concepts in psychology for two reasons. First, it has been shown to be important in all areas including mental health, physical health, sports, music, entertainment, art, education, medicine, and business.

Second, whereas it may be harder to change your ability or the amount of experience you have doing something, it may be easier to boost your self-efficacy.

Think about that. We said that perseverance and grit can be great equalizers. Self-efficacy may often be an even greater equalizer. Do you know the story of when Susan Boyle went on *Britain's Got Talent* to sing before Simon Cowell and the other hyper-critical judges? She sang *I Dreamed a Dream* from *Les Misérables*. The beauty of her singing blew everyone away – including Simon Cowell! It took an incredible amount of self-efficacy – belief in her ability to sing in front of those people – to do it and she was richly rewarded for succeeding.

Before I tell you what you can do to increase your self-efficacy for reaching your goals, I want to first tell you what research has shown about why it is so important.

First, self-efficacy makes us more likely to approach a difficult task or goal as a challenge to be mastered rather than a threat to be avoided. In other words, we may be more likely to have a growth mindset that we can learn even if we fail rather than a fixed mindset in thinking that we are just not cut out for it.

Second, self-efficacy makes us set more challenging goals and stay committed to them. It is hard to imagine a more challenging goal than making the most of our life and living it to the fullest like we are focusing on here.

Third, self-efficacy can enable us to take a broader view of our lives and increase our creativity by giving us more options and ways to succeed. We will be more likely to see the big picture that includes the rewards rather than just what we are afraid of.

Fourth, in Chapter 5, there was a special video that showed an extraordinary example of resilience when a young woman running a race fell and got up to win the race. Another reason that self-efficacy makes us more successful is that it enables us to do the kind of thing that she dared to try to do even after she fell.

Fifth, and this is the reason that we may least expect, self-efficacy makes us more successful because it reduces the stress and emotional distress we experience while engaged in a challenging activity. When we have the self-efficacy to believe that we will be successful, we literally won't sweat it as much.

So, these are the reasons why self-efficacy is so important and one of the greatest contributions of modern psychology to successful functioning and having a good life. But the next thing may be one of the most valuable lessons that we can ever learn and it has to do with what we can do to increase our self-efficacy. I often say to my students that even if they need to fall asleep for most of the classes during the semester, this is one time that they may want to be sure to be awake. There has been excellent research on what we can do to boost self-efficacy and it boils down to these five things.

The first is called "performance experiences." For many of us, the best way to increase our confidence is simply to practice performing the task we want to master or something close to it. Even the smallest success on a similar task can increase our self-efficacy. The other principle that can help in using performance experiences to build self-efficacy is to break down complex and challenging tasks into simpler "baby steps" that can be practiced and mastered one at a time.

The second way to increase self-efficacy is simply to watch or see someone else successfully working towards the same kind of goal that we have. This could be watching a good friend or family member, reading about a sports hero or famous person in history, or even reading or watching fictional stories. If you have lost your parents, when you see an orphan like Harry Potter come to believe in himself after he lost his – you are building your own self-efficacy.

The third way to increase self-efficacy is to imagine ourselves doing what it takes to reach our ultimate goal. But if we want to win a big fight like the movie character Rocky, it is not so much imagining ourselves winning the fight as it is imagining ourselves getting up early on a cold morning and running up and down those stairs. During the last part of this challenge, we are going to give you some wonderful tools you can use to increase your self-efficacy for creating a better future. Part of why they have been so effective is that they boost your self-efficacy by getting you to imagine a better future and what you can do to make it happen.

The fourth way to increase self-efficacy brings us back to the idea of strength in numbers that we talked about with resilience. This fourth way is to get positive feedback from others who encourage us in what we are doing in working toward our goal. This encouragement is most effective if it comes from someone we look up to and who knows about what we are trying to do - and they may be easier to find than you think. During the last part of this challenge, we will help you identify and enlist the kind of people who can do this for you.

The fifth and final way to increase self-efficacy brings us back to the connection between self-efficacy and our physiological state of stress or relaxation. Just as having self-efficacy leads to reduced emotional distress during a challenge, so too can decreasing our distress lead to an increase in self-efficacy. If you can simply use mindful breathing or one of the many other relaxation techniques available, you will automatically be increasing your self-efficacy as you become less anxious and more relaxed.

Thus, these five ways to increase self-efficacy may be one of the most important things for us to remember and try for ourselves. Self-efficacy is the belief that we can do what it takes to reach our goals – and doing these things will not only increase that belief but also the likelihood that we will be successful.

Workbook Tasks for the Chapter

Here are the tasks that will help you better understand the power of self-efficacy, how to increase it, and how to use your strengths to reach your goals.

First, as after every chapter, there is a link to a video where you can see and hear me going over the lesson for this chapter.

Second, there is a video of an amazing young man who despite having no limbs, being bullied for years, and contemplating suicide; went on to believe in himself and become an inspiration to people around the world. You will be asked to reflect on how self-efficacy may have enabled him to do what he does and how just seeing him do it and learning about his story may affect your self-efficacy.

Third, there is a reflection question about a time you were at your best when your self-efficacy was high and what may have made it high for you. Identifying these kinds of experiences and reflecting on them will help you understand why self-efficacy can be so important and what may be some of the best ways for you to foster it.

Fourth, there is a writing task that asks you to identify a goal or area of your life where you would like to increase your self-efficacy. After you identify it, the next step is to write about how you might use one or more of the five ways to increase self-efficacy you learned about to do it. Since one of the five ways involves imagining yourself doing what it takes to reach an important goal, you will be increasing your self-efficacy just by doing the task.

Fifth, there is another task that involves using one of your top strengths in a new way, but this time you are asked to use it to reach one of your goals for the future. The first part of the task involves brainstorming about how you might be able to use your strengths to create a better future and the second part involves doing one of the things you come up with and seeing what happens.

1. Author's Video for this Chapter

Here is the link for the video of me going over the lesson for this chapter.

https://youtu.be/zHlEEC_kwgU

2. Special Video – "The Most Inspirational Video You Will Ever See - Nick Vujicic's Story"

Watch the video and reflect on how self-efficacy may have enabled Nick to do what he does without arms or legs and how seeing what he does may affect your self-efficacy for doing different things.

https://www.youtube.com/watch?v=Q6HnFuzSJdQ

3. Reflection Question

What is a time you were at your best when you think that your self-efficacy was particularly high (e.g., you were very confident that you would be successful)? Why do you think your self-efficacy was so high? Which of the five ways of increasing self-efficacy may have helped you increase yours?

___

___

4. Increasing Your Self-Efficacy

Identify a goal or area of your life where you would like to increase your self-efficacy and write about how you could use one or more of the five ways to increase it.

5. Using Your Top Strengths in New Ways to Reach Your Goals

This activity involves thinking about how you can use your top strengths to create a better future and then doing something to use one of these strengths to make progress in reaching a future goal. The first step is to brainstorm about what you may be able to do and the second step is to try one of the things you think about and write about what happened.

What are some ways that you can use your top strengths to reach a future goal?

Which of the ways that you identified would you most like to try? When and where can you do it?

____

____

____

____

____

____

What did you do to use one of your top strengths to reach one of your goals for the future? How well did it work? What role do you think that self-efficacy may have played in how well it worked?

____

____

____

____

____

____

____

____

____

Chapter 12

Self-Control

If you learn self-control, you can master anything.
— Unknown

Do you remember how earlier in this part of the challenge I talked about that sailboat metaphor? Do you remember I compared fixing the holes in the boat to working on our weaknesses and lifting the sails to using our top strengths? I can imagine that for many the lesson of this chapter may involve paying attention to some of those holes.

Despite the fact that it is a top strength for some people, self-control, which is also known as self-regulation, is consistently one of the lowest strengths when you average across all people around the world. What's more, you can see how it could be quite a gaping hole for some of us - and may cause us to take on too much water and run aground before we even get started!

But never fear – or at least never let that fear keep you from trying. Just as with self-efficacy, I have some good news. There have been many promising discoveries about self-control and how we can increase it.

First of all, just what is self-control? It has recently been compared to "willpower" by the psychologist Roy Baumeister, who has probably done the most to advance its study in the past 20 years. He defined self-control as the conscious and deliberate effort to control: (1) thoughts – like getting rid of doubts about ourselves or our ability to succeed; (2) feelings – like not hastily reacting in anger in traffic; (3) impulses – like not eating the rest of that chocolate cake; and (4) performance – like hitting the right notes on the piano or going for a record on that video game we love.

The classic experiment that demonstrated the importance of self-control is what has been called the "marshmallow experiment", of which you will see a delightful example of in the special video for this chapter. This experiment was first conducted at Stanford University in the 1960s when 4-year-old boys and girls were left alone by themselves in a room with one big marshmallow on the table right in front of them. Before they were left alone, the experimenter told them that they could eat the marshmallow now or, if they did not eat it before the experimenter returned, they could have another marshmallow.

After the experimenter leaves the room, a camera films what the kids do. Their facial expressions and what they do to deal with this mild form of torture is priceless for the way it shows us some of what we all do in the face of temptation. The first result of the experiment was that a significant portion of the kids quickly ate that first marshmallow, sometimes before the experimenter could even finish the instructions. In addition, there was another significant portion of the kids who waited the 10-15 minutes that must have seemed like an eternity for that second marshmallow.

But the most remarkable thing about the findings is what the experimenters discovered when they followed up with the four-year-olds 14 years later. They found that those in what the experimenters called the "waiter group" were doing much better than those in what they called the "grabber group." Specifically, those that waited for that second marshmallow were better copers, more socially competent, self-assertive, trustworthy, dependable, and better able to resist temptation as teenagers.

In addition, the "waiters" were better able to control themselves when things didn't go their way, more able to focus on their studies, did better in school, and had significantly higher college entrance exam scores. In addition to these initial studies with young children, there have been numerous studies showing how important self-control may be for everything from mental and physical health to success at school, work, and in relationships.

The positive part of the psychology of self-control is that there is so much we can do to strengthen it. The psychologist Roy Baumeister has compared self-control to a muscle that anyone – no matter how big this particular hole is in their sailboat – can exercise and strengthen just as we can our biceps and triceps. As with the ways we can increase self-efficacy that were presented in the last chapter, what we know about how to increase self-control may be some of the most important, powerful, and relevant lessons that modern psychology has discovered for us.

Here are the five ways we know the most about that have been shown to increase our self-control. The first is simply called "self-monitoring." Most people don't know that it is responsible for more than half of the success of some of the hardest things we try to do – like losing weight. It is simply noting on paper, a computer, or a smart phone that you did something you wanted to do, or that you didn't do something that you didn't want to do. This simple noting of how you are doing with your self-control goal can make a big difference in getting you to exercise it and in how successful you are in actually doing it.

Second, and I'm sure that this combination of big words probably got someone who studied this tenure, is what is called "implementation intention." This involves setting a goal for increasing self-control, like not having a hot fudge sundae at Baskin Robbins on your way home from work. Next, you develop a plan for what to do when faced with potential obstacles, like seeing a new ice cream store on your alternate way home! This may involve practicing what you will do or say to yourself when you hear that little voice saying that one more triple-dip sundae won't hurt that much - just this one time.

The third way to increase self-control is called "mental contrasting" and this involves three steps. The first is to identify an important change that you want to make. The second is to identify and imagine the most positive and successful outcome that may result from the change. The third is to add the part from the implementation intention about imagining the obstacles that may stand in the way of you reaching your goal. In other words, envision your goal and its benefits and then mentally walk through the obstacles to achieving it.

The fourth way to increase self-control is one that I'm sure most of us have done at some point but may have felt like it was cheating. In reality, it may be one of the only things that work at first. It is called "stimulus control" but could just as easily be called something less technical like "out of sight, out of mind." It involves keeping yourself physically distant from the liquor store or not keeping alcohol in your house, or staying psychologically distant by singing your favorite song to keep you from thinking about that triple-dip sundae.

The final way to increase self-control has by far my favorite name and is called "urge surfing." It turns out that if we have a strong craving for something, trying to put it out of our mind may not always work. There is a famous experiment where people were asked not to think about a white bear, and the harder they tried not to think about it, the more they actually thought about it. Anyway, urge surfing is a skill that involves mindfully observing a craving and watching it rise and fall like a big wave at the beach. Whereas you may have thought it would never go away, if you hold off long enough from grabbing that marshmallow, you learn that the craving actually does recede and, in the process, you gain more control and ability to resist the temptation to eat before you can get another.

So, there are five things that we can all do to increase self-control – and give us the discipline and willpower we need to reach out goals and avoid some of those temptations that get in the way.

Workbook Tasks for the Chapter

The tasks focus on understanding the value of self-control, savoring, and the relationship of savoring with self-control, and how to foster them both:

First, as after every chapter, there is a link to a video where you can see and hear me going over the lesson for this chapter.

Second, there is a special video of the marshmallow experiment where you are asked to see if you can identify something in what the children do that you have done in trying to exercise self-control. Watching this video can be a way to better understand the many ways that we all try to resist temptation and how imperfect we often are in actually doing it!

Third, you will be asked to identify an area in your life where you would most like to improve your self-control and write about how you can use one of the five ways you learned about to do it. The idea is for you to write about something that may be particularly challenging because just writing about it may help you gain the self-efficacy or belief in yourself that you may need to actually do it.

Fourth, there is an activity that involves savoring, which can reduce our need to exercise self-control by increasing our enjoyment of some of the things we may need to try to control. For example, if we learn to savor the taste of our favorite chocolate for a longer period of time, we won't need to eat as much to get the same enjoyment from it.

Fifth, there are reflection questions about the areas of your life where exercising more self-control might bring the greatest benefits and what you would most like to savor in the future. Imagining the rewards of exercising self-control and the benefits of savoring will increase your motivation for doing both and make it more likely that you will do them.

Finally, I wanted to congratulate you. You have almost made it to the end of the second part of this challenge. You may have had more self-control than you thought! The goal of this part was for you to better see, appreciate, and use what is best in yourself and begin to experience more of what it might be like for you to lift the sails and feel the wind at your back in using it.

In the next part, we will build on your basic training and what you learned in this part to make it come to life in your relationships with others and the world around you. In the fourth and final part after that, we will bring try to put it all together in enabling you to develop a plan for continuing to use what you have been learning to create the kind of life you seek and that would make you most happy.

1. Author Video for this Lesson

Here is the link for the video of me going over the lesson for this chapter.

https://youtu.be/t2TtNgrGYbY

2. Special Video – "Marshmallow Test – (funny)"

Watch the video and see if you can identify something in what the children do that you have also done to try to exercise self-control.

https://www.youtube.com/watch?v=Sc4EF3ijVJ8

3. Increasing Self-Control

Identify an area in your life where you would most like to increase self-control and write about how you could use at least one of the five ways presented in the lesson to do it.

____

____

____

____

____

____

4. Savoring

Write down five things that you would like to take time to savor and then savor one of them for at least five minutes after spending a few minutes practicing mindful breathing.

1. ____________________

2. ____________________

3. ____________________

4. ____________________

5. ____________________

What did you savor? What was it like to do it? How was the experience the same or different from what you expected?

____

____

____

____

____

____

____

5. Reflection Questions

What is an area of your life where there may be the greatest benefits for exercising more self-control? Write about the benefits, what they might feel like to do, and how they might change your life.

____

____

____

____

____

____

____

What would you most like to take more time to savor in the future? When, where, and how can you take time to do this?

Part 3 – Bringing Out the Best around You

What is this part about?

Purpose: The purpose of this part is to enable you to improve your relationships and have a more beneficial and rewarding involvement with and positive impact on others and the world around you.

Topics: There are chapters about the value of social intelligence; how to increase love, kindness, and work for the greater good; and on fostering the justice and forgiveness we need in order to happy and live well together.

Activities: The most important activities focus on finding new ways to express love and kindness with both friends and strangers and learning how to be involved with causes you care about and that can bring joy and meaning to your life.

Chapter 13

Social Intelligence

When someone shows you who they are,
Believe them the first time.
— Maya Angelou

Welcome to the third part of the positive psychology challenge! Let's do a quick review of what we have done so far.

In the first part, you had basic training about positive psychology as the science of happiness and what makes life worth living. You learned about happiness and well-being, including PERMA theory, which says that there may be at least five things we seek for their own sake: positive emotions, engagement, relationships, meaning, and accomplishment.

You also learned about what can help make these five things more a part of our lives and make positive change possible. These included the basic building blocks of positive reappraisal, behavioral activation, and gradually exposing ourselves to what we are afraid of. They also included mindfulness, as what enables us to more present to our lives; resilience and stress-related growth, as what help us bounce back and benefit from stress; and wisdom and creativity, which can help us find our way in stressful and uncertain times. The primary activity you did variations of during several chapters involved learning to see and create more good things in your life.

In the second part of the challenge, you had an opportunity to discover and learn how to better use what is best in you. You learned about authenticity as being true to ourselves; perseverance and its' cousins grit and growth mindset; courage as what enables us to overcome obstacles; self-efficacy as believing that we can do what it takes to reach our goals; and self-control, which is like a muscle that we can exercise to strengthen. The primary activity you did during most of the chapters in the second part involved identifying your strengths and discovering new ways to use them.

During this third part of the challenge, we will focus on how you can use your strengths and what you are learning to improve your relationships and have more of a positive impact on the world around you. In the fourth and final part of this challenge, we provide the lessons and activities which will enable you to put what you have been learning together and use it as a foundation in planning for a better future. Since the focus in this third part is on improving your relationships and better engaging with the larger community and world around you, the lessons will involve the activities, attitudes, behaviors, and strengths that will make this possible.

In this chapter, we'll begin by focusing on social intelligence as a foundation for interacting with those around us. The next two chapters will be about fostering love and kindness, followed by chapters on improving the larger community and building a healthy society, and ending with a chapter on forgiveness as a way to find peace and healing when things go awry in our relationships. The primary focus for the activities in this third part will be on doing things that improve your relationships with others and with the larger groups and communities of which you are a part.

The critical lesson for this third part of the challenge might be summed up in the words of Chris Peterson that "other people matter" and the words of the John Donne that "no man (or "no person" in modern terms) is an island." That is, human beings need each other, and our destiny is intricately tied to those around us.

The psychologist Ed Diener has probably done more to study happiness around the world than anyone else. He has asked people of all ages, genders, ethnic groups, languages, and cultures what makes them happy. The common denominator is having and being with other people they care about and who care about them. In fact, when asked to describe when they were happiest, Diener says that people almost always described times when they were enjoying themselves with close friends or family members.

The vital importance of our relationships is strongly reflected in our biology and evolution as a species. As I previously noted, our intelligence did not evolve to do higher math or physics, but to enable us to get along with others and successfully negotiate our social world. That is why our intelligence may be best characterized as the "social intelligence" that it takes to build and maintain trusting, supportive, and rewarding relationships with other people and the larger community.

The thing that has the strongest correlation with the size of our brains compared with other species of primates is the size of our social network. The anthropologist Robin Dunbar showed that human beings have both the largest brain size and the largest social network while other primates with smaller brains have correspondingly smaller networks. More than anything, we need our intelligence to build and maintain good relationships.

There are other discoveries about our biology that also highlight the significance of our relationships with others. First, there are parts of our brains that have specifically evolved to play a role in social intelligence, such as the fusiform gyrus which enables us to recognize facial expressions in others. Second, our brains have what have been called mirror neurons that react both when we perform an action and when we see another person perform the same action. Mirror neurons enable us to learn from and understand the actions and experiences of others. Third, we have a powerful hormone called oxytocin, which is associated with social bonding and is more active when we are close or even think about being close to others. Fourth, in addition to our "fight-or-flight" response to stress, we also have a slower acting response called the "tend-or-befriend" response that involves oxytocin and motivates us to take care of and befriend others when we are under stress.

One of the most advanced aspects of our social intelligence involves what has been called "theory of mind." Rather than being a particular theory of how our minds generally work, theory of mind refers to the fact that we are constantly developing working theories about how those around us are going to behave and what they are going to do next. It is not hard to see how important it might be for us to be able to know whether we can trust those around us. This may have been a critical survival skill in our evolutionary past as it still can be today. Our fascination with a good murder mystery or reality TV show about who will end up with the bachelor or the bachelorette are a testament to how good we are at theory of mind, how important it is for us, and how much we enjoy developing and using it.

The bottom line of these discoveries in psychology and science is that our relationships and engagement with the larger community are essential for surviving, thriving, and flourishing – and that is why it is the central focus of this part of the challenge. In the chapters of this part, you will learn what science has discovered about love and kindness, how our happiness is related to the health of the community around us, how to make moral and ethical choices that promote a healthy community, and what we can do to foster the forgiveness that is sometimes necessary to sustain it. In the process, you will learn about some of the most effective and promising ways to improve your relationships as well as how to have more of a positive impact on the community and world around you.

The activities for this part of the challenge are grounded in two things that are essential for healthy and life-giving relationships with others. First, it is important for us to experience and express appreciation and gratitude for the meaning and happiness others bring to our lives. Second, the primary behaviors that foster good relationships include love, kindness, and treating each other with fairness and justice and also with empathy and compassion. The tasks and activities will focus on providing you with ways to use what you are learning to better relate to others and engage with the world around you.

Workbook Tasks for the Chapter

Here are the tasks that can help you better understand and increase your social intelligence:

First, as after every chapter, there is a link to a video where you can see and hear me going over the lesson for this chapter.

Second, there is a special video about "Active Constructive Responding," which is a way of responding to someone when they have good news to tell us about something that has happened to them. It was originally studied by psychologist Shelly Gable and has been shown to produce better and more lasting relationships. It can be a simple, fun, and easy thing to practice for improving our relationships. After you watch the video, you will be asked who you can practice it with in the near future and what it was like to practice.

Third, there is an activity that involves making a list of the people in your life you are most grateful for and writing down something about why you are grateful for each of them. This will be a way to prepare you for other tasks that involve focusing on what you appreciate about other people and writing and sharing a gratitude letter with someone who has been important to you.

Fourth, there is a task that involves completing a special form about what you appreciate in someone who you may be particularly grateful for. Completing this form will help you gain a better understanding of why this person is important to you and what you can do to improve your relationship. Then you will be asked to make and carry out a plan to do something to improve it.

Finally, there are reflection questions about who has been a good mentor or guide for you and who you have been a good mentor or guide for. This can help you see why both having and being a mentor can be so important for us.

1. Author's Video for this Lesson

Here is the link for the video of me going over the lesson for this chapter.

https://youtu.be/PxI6jFYcGA4

2. Special Video – "Active Constructive Responding"

Watch the video and answer the questions below about who you can practice with and what is most important to remember in practicing it.

https://www.youtube.com/watch?v=qRORihbXMnA

Who could you practice Active Constructive Responding with in the near future?

____

____

____

After you get the chance to practice it, how did the other person or persons react? How did do feel when you were doing it and how do you think it affected your relationship?

____

____

____

____

____

3. Who Are You Grateful For?

Make a list of the people in your life you are most grateful for. Write down something about why you are grateful to each of them.

4. Relationship Appreciative Inquiry

Complete the "Relationship Appreciative Inquiry" questions (see Appendix H) for at least one person currently in your life. Completing this inquiry will help you gain a better understanding of why they are important to you. As you answer these questions, think about what you might be able to do in the near future to improve your relationship with them. After you complete the form, make and carry out a plan in the near future to improve that relationship. After you complete the Relationship Appreciate Inquiry form, answer the following questions:

Who did you focus on for the Relationship Appreciative Inquiry? What are some things you can do to try to improve the relationship?

___

___

___

___

___

___

___

___

___

___

___

___

___

___

Answer these questions after you get the chance to do something to improve your relationship: What did you do? What happened and how did it affect both of you?

5. Reflection Questions

Who has been a good mentor or guide for you and what have you learned from them??

Who has you been a good mentor or guide for you and what do you think they have you learned from you?

Chapter 14

Love

The things that matter most in our lives are not fantastic or grand.
They are moments when we touch one another.
— Jack Kornfield

In this chapter, I will talk about the different kinds of love we experience and that bring joy and meaning to our relationships. Just as we learned in the last chapter that social intelligence may be the primary focus of our intelligence, so the experience of love may be the heart of our relationships and provide a foundation for much of our happiness.

The psychologist John Lee did a comprehensive study of the use of the word "love" in history and literature and identified six different kinds of love, or what he calls "love styles." These include:

1. Eros - the passionate sexual love where a lover idealizes a partner.
2. Ludus - love that is short on commitment and played as a game.
3. Storge - the kind of mutual affection shared between friends.
4. Pragma - a pragmatic, practical, and mutually beneficial relationship.
5. Mania - a dramatic, stormy relationship with cycles of jealousy and breakups.
6. Agape - a self-giving love where one is fully concerned with the welfare of the other.

People may debate whether the game playing Ludus or the stormy Mania may really make us happy or are good for us, but the other four love styles do consistently appear to play an important role in our happiness and well-being. These four are highlighted in much current theory and research on love and relationships. While some people doubt whether a completely self-giving love such as Agape is common; many see it in the sacrificial love of a parent or grandparent for a child, or even in the devotion of a teacher to their students, coaches to their players, or someone in a helping profession to those they serve.

In contrast, you can see aspects of the other three elements of Eros, Storge, and Pragma in other research and theory about adult romantic relationships. The psychologist Robert Sternberg developed what he called the Triangular theory of love where the three important components of love include Passion, which is similar to Lee's Eros; Intimacy, which is similar to Lee's Storge; and Commitment, which includes aspects of Lee's Pragma and Agape. Sternberg thinks that the quality of love we experience depends on the relative strength of these three components. In addition, although it may be difficult to find and sustain all three in the same relationship over time, they may still be a worthwhile goal.

Psychologists Ellen Berscheid and Elaine Hatfield have studied the usual course of Eros (in both Lee and Sternberg's terms), which they call Passionate Love; and Storge (in Lee's terms) or Intimacy (in Sternberg's terms), which they call Companionate Love in romantic relationships. They compare Passionate Love to a fire that heats up and cools down quickly and Companionate Love to the intertwining of branches that continue to grow together.

Berscheid and Hatfield think people often make one of two mistakes in the early stages of romantic relationships. The first mistake is to make a commitment too soon during an early peak of Passionate Love. The second is to break-up too soon after Passionate Love naturally begins to fall from its' initially intense and high level. In both instances, the couple may not wait long enough to see if it will be possible for Companionate Love to take root and grow. Therefore, being aware of and placing more value on Companionate Love may be a key to preventing these mistakes and improving many romantic relationships.

Aside from adult romantic relationships, the other most valued and important context for love is lasting, close relationships with friends and family member. Although the focus here is not necessarily on a romantic relationship, it does involve what Lee calls Storge, Sternberg calls Intimacy, and Berscheid and Hatfield call Companionate Love. When I have asked students in class which is more important to them, there is always 30-40% who say Eros or Passionate Love but the consistent and clear majority of both women and men have put Companionate Love or friendship at the top of their list.

There is another focus for love that has often been neglected in modern cultures that have idealized self-sacrifice and self-giving forms of love. There has been a lot of recent research showing the value of a form of self-love that has been called "self-compassion" or "self-kindness." This kind of self-love does not involve the self-inflation and lack of empathy associated with narcissism but rather accepts and embraces our weakness, limitations, and imperfections as part of our common humanity. This kind of self-love appears to be particularly beneficial for caregivers, people who are vulnerable to compassion fatigue, and those who suffer various forms of oppression and/or discrimination.

In putting all of this together, the growing body of theory and research on human love points to the value of at least four kinds of loving relationships for our happiness and well-being: (1) romantic relationships, (2) close friendships, (3) relationships where we are taught or mentored by or teach or mentor another (similar to Lee's self-giving Agape), and (4) a relationship with ourselves characterized by the kindness, and compassion that accepts and embraces ourselves for all of who we are, with both our strengths and our weaknesses.

In finishing this lesson on love, I want to leave you with some things that may enable you to improve your relationships, especially close relationships with partners, friends, and family members. After years of studying couples and seeing what predicts their staying together or separating, the psychologist John Gottman has literally written the book on what enables people to stay together and thrive in their relationships. Here are the seven principles that he has identified for making a relationship last.

1. Enhance your love map – become familiar with your partner, friend, or family member's world including their worries, hopes, goals, and strengths.
2. Nurture fondness and admiration – by meditating on what you love, appreciate, and

cherish in them (as was a goal of the "Relationship Appreciative Inquiry" that was a task in the Chapter 13).

3. Turn towards them – be there for them through big and small events and give them affection and support when they ask for it.
4. Accept influence – share power with them by deciding things together and taking their feelings into account.
5. Solve solvable problems – learn to resolve problems and conflicts with tolerance and compromise to prevent negative feelings from escalating.
6. Overcome gridlock – when stuck in a conflict, be patient in exploring the issues that may have caused the gridlock by letting it sit for now and coming back to it later.
7. Create shared meaning – create rituals and symbols that you can continue to share using things like pictures, videos, or songs that express important parts of your relationship.

In addition to these, I would add the Active Constructive Responding that was the focus of the special video in Chapter 13. As the video explained, this involves responding to good news with empathy, enthusiasm, and asking for elaboration and finding ways to celebrate with them. Research has shown that Active Constructive Responding produces better and longer lasting relationships than other ways of responding to good news.

The last thing to do in this lesson is help you think about the different ways that people give and receive love in their close relationships. The author Gary Chapman identified what he calls five different Languages of Love. You will have the chance to take a survey for this chapter to help you see which of the following languages you prefer:

1. Words of affirmation – it involves encouraging, affirming, and appreciating another.
2. Physical touch – the non-verbal use of body language and touch to show love.
3. Receiving gifts – thoughtful gifts and gestures to show gratitude for someone.
4. Quality time – uninterrupted and focused conversations and time together.
5. Acts of service – doing chores, errands, and other things to lighten someone's load.

Before we finish our lesson on love, it is important to note that while the VIA classification has identified and defined love as a strength, there are things we may call "love" (e.g., such as Ludus and Mania in Lee's terms) that may not always foster happiness and well-being. When trying to understand the role of love in our happiness and well-being, it is particularly important to be clear about what kind of "love" we are talking about. But even with this caution about some of what we may call love, there is little doubt that the forms that involve mutual giving and support are often one of our greatest sources of joy, happiness, meaning, and fulfillment. We hope that this challenge will enable you to find new ways to express love in the forms that best bring each of these more into your life.

Workbook Tasks for the Chapter

Here are the tasks designed to help you understand, recognize, and improve your ability to give, receive, and benefit from love in your life:

First, as after every chapter, there is a link to a video where you can see and hear me going over the lesson for this chapter.

Second, there is a special video called Love Liberates by Maya Angelou and you are asked to think about how love may have liberated you and how you could love someone else in a way that might liberate them.

Third, there are reflection questions asking you to identify and write about one of the best loving or kind acts that someone has done for you. You are also asked to think about how it has affected you and how you can give back or honor what was done for you.

Fourth, we want you to write a letter expressing your gratitude to someone you have not fully or properly thanked. Ideally, it would be someone you could read or send it too and you would share it as soon as you can in the near future. Research has shown that this can be a powerful way to increase our happiness. While there are many ways that you can continue to express gratitude to the people you come across in your life, writing a letter like this and sharing it has been a great way for many people to get started.

Fifth, we want you to take the Languages of Love survey to identify the language(s) that you prefer and think about how knowing what you prefer may enable you to better give and receive love. This will help you better understand the different ways that people often try to express love and how sometimes we completely miss expressions we don't understand.

1. Author Video for this Lesson

Here is the link for the video of me going over the lesson for this chapter.

https://youtu.be/D7igjMBjqSk

2. Special Video – "Dr. Maya Angelou – Love Liberates"

Watch the video and reflect on how love may have liberated you and how you could love someone else in a way that might liberate them.

https://www.youtube.com/watch?v=cbecKv2xR14&t=89s

3. Reflection Questions

What is one of the best acts of kindness, compassion, or love that anyone has done for you? Be specific about what they did and why it may have been important to you

____

____

How has the act that you describe affected you? What could you do to give back or honor what they did for you?

4. Gratitude Letter

Think of a person who you have not fully or properly thanked. If possible, try to identify someone you could personally thank in the near future. Then write a letter expressing your gratitude. Next, read or share your letter with them in as personal a way as you can. You may want to use the following space to write all or part of your letter and/or save it in another private place. You could also use the space below to write about what it was like for you to write your letter, share it with the other person, how they responded, and what you learned from doing it.

5. Languages of Love Survey

Take the Languages of Love survey to identify your preferred languages of love and answer the question below.

https://www.5lovelanguages.com/quizzes/

How might understanding your language of love enable you to better give and receive love with those who are most important to you?

Chapter 15

Kindness

Be kind, for everyone you meet is fighting a hard battle.

— Philo

So far in this third part of the challenge, we have focused on social intelligence because of the central place that relationships have in our lives and on love because it is so often a part of what makes us happy and our lives worth living.

In this chapter, we will begin focusing less on our immediate relationships and what we receive from others, and more on how we can have a positive impact on both those we know and love and also on strangers in the larger world beyond. Research has consistently shown that kindness can play a primary role in increasing our happiness and well-being. Kindness is one of those things that many people say they value greatly and that we can't exercise enough. However, it is also something that some people think may not always be a good thing and could even hurt us or be a sign of weakness.

Actually, kindness is at the very heart of this challenge and for many people may be the thing that has the most potential for changing our lives for the better. There is a popular foreign movie where the main character decides to do the same experiment that we hope you will try for this part of the challenge. The script for the movie was written by a director who had enough previous success that he had earned the opportunity to do something that was meaningful and close to his heart. He wrote a script that included as many of the extraordinary acts of kindness that he had seen across the years as possible – all centered around the main character. After it was released in 2001, the movie was nominated for five Academy Awards and won an award for the best European screenplay.

The name of the movie is *Amélie* and it was about a girl in Paris named Amélie. Amélie grew up as the lonely and neglected only child of parents who were completely self-absorbed and could not relate to her. Her world changed one day when as a lonely young adult she found a box of childhood treasures in her bedroom wall. She decided to try to find the person that the treasure box had belonged to and made a deal with herself about it. If she was able to find the person and it had a positive impact on them, then she would change her life. She would continue to be kind in as many ways as she could.

Without spoiling too much of the movie if you haven't seen it, her initial experiment was a success and the rest of the movie is about how her acts of kindness ripple out to change the lives of the people around her. Moreover, her kindness also brings her what she most wanted and most feared – an intimate relationship with a man she came to love in trying to be kind to him. If you remember in the second part of this challenge, I said I hoped you would begin to feel the wind at your back the way that Stevie Wonder did when he came to really appreciate his gift for hearing. In this chapter, I want to add my hope that you might do the same type of experiment Amélie did and be surprised by the same kind of joy.

One of the most promising and encouraging findings in positive psychology is the confirmation and support of what Amélie discovered and what we all can too. Acts of kindness have tremendous potential for increasing happiness and well-being – both for those we are kind to and for ourselves. Some of you may have already experienced this, while others may be a bit more skeptical.

Before I go any farther, I want to say something about why kindness may be such a potent catalyst for happiness and positive change – and I also want to say something about how it may have sometimes gotten a bad name. There seem to be two overarching ways that kindness may benefit us.

First, being kind to people we know or can have a relationship with generally results in an upward spiral of reciprocal giving, where we increasingly get something back from others. It is karma with a big K.

Second, kindness enables us to feel good about ourselves. We come to see ourselves as someone who can have a positive impact on others and make a difference to world around us. Good karma is great but this is probably the main reason that Amélie changed – and this is where kindness can be a real source of transformation even when we don't expect or get anything in return. On the wall of Mother Teresa's room in Calcutta, there was reported to be a sentence about kindness that said – "if you are kind, people may accuse you of ulterior motives… be kind anyway."

This form of kindness to strangers or to those who can't or don't give back to us can be extremely powerful. No matter what anyone has done to us, we can still choose to be kind. This is what Nelson Mandela did when he was in prison for so long and it won the hearts of the prison guards who came to admire and respect him so much. This is the kind of power that Gandhi and Martin Luther King, Jr. discovered and embraced that made reconciliation, healing, and social change happen where it before had seemed impossible.

But if kindness can come back to us through those we know and can also empower us in unforeseen ways, then why does it sometimes get a bad name? Why aren't people kind more often? The main reason may be that we often mistake kindness for an imposter. This imposter can be seen in the distinction made between what might be called "naïve kindness" and "wise kindness." Naïve kindness is when we do something that may look or seem nice not because it is best for another person, but because we want to be liked or are afraid to do what might really be most kind and best for the other person.

In contrast, wise kindness is like the "Jedi saber" that Jesus flashed when he told those who were about to stone the woman who had been caught committing adultery – "Let he who is without sin cast the first stone." Although it may not have felt like kindness at the time to those in the crowd who dropped the stones one at a time and left; it may have been quite kind in calling forth the "better angels of their nature" to use Abraham Lincoln's phrase - and it certainly would feel profoundly kind to that woman who was set free and got a second chance to live.

Which brings us back to the story of Amélie and the last big plot twist in this chapter about kindness. Before Amélie could really be transformed and sustain her desire to be the beacon of kindness that she fantasized about becoming, she needed to allow someone else to love her – and thereby become happy in filling her own cup. This brings us back to why it might be important for us to make a list of those we are grateful for and make sure there are those on our list who see us and love us for who we are.

For now, more than anything else that we ask you to do in this challenge, we want to encourage you to carry out the same kind of bold experiment that Amélie did in the movie. Give yourself the chance to find the ways you can become like that Jedi knight, that black belt master, that virtuoso - but not at playing the violin. Instead, become a master at doing things you enjoy in using your own strengths to bring your own unique expression of kindness to those around you. Then, like Amélie, just wait and see what happens.

Workbook Tasks for the Chapter

Here are the tasks that will help you understand and appreciate the power of kindness and find more ways to practice and experience its benefits:

First of all, as after every chapter, there is a link to a video where you can see and hear me going over the lesson for this chapter.

Second, there is a special video on The Power of Kindness by Johann Berlin where he talks about why kindness may be so important and how we might best practice it.

Third, there is an activity that involves going through a list of many different kind acts and identifying new ones that you would most like to try. Reviewing comprehensive lists like this can be a good way to become more creative in finding new ways to be kind and in expressing our top strengths and what we really enjoy doing in being kind.

Fourth, the next activity builds on the review of the list of kind acts by asking you to make a top ten list of kind acts you would most like to try for someone you already know and another top ten list of kind acts you would most like to try for a stranger.

Fifth, the last activity involves trying one of the new kind acts that you identified for someone you know and answering questions about what happened. This is a way of beginning to do the same kind of experiment that Amélie did in the movie and that we focused on in this chapter.

1. Author's Video for this Lesson

Here is the link for the video of me going over the lesson for this chapter.

https://youtu.be/P7lnMXdEbNQ

2. Special Video – "The power of kindness: Johann Berlin"

Watch this special video on the power of kindness and think about what it might be calling you to do and what impact it may have on the person or persons who are the recipients of your kindness – and also think about what impact it may have on you.

https://www.youtube.com/watch?v=CG-SmD5X5Kk

3. Identifying Acts of Kindness

Because we so easily fall into a rut in thinking there are only a few ways to be kind, we want you to read through the whole list of the Acts of Kindness Planner (see Appendix I). As you do, put a letter in the "To Try" column to indicate the acts you would most like to try. Be sure to include acts that you can do for both people you already know and for strangers. Put an "A" for those you would most like to try, a "B" for those that aren't quite as high on your list, and a "C" for those you would like to consider again at some point.

In the future, after you have tried any of those that you check, there are also columns where you can put in a grade (A, B, C, D, etc.) to indicate how much of a positive impact you think doing the kind act had on you (the "On Self" column) and on any others that the kind act was direct towards or any others who were affected (the "On Other" column).

4. Planning Acts of Kindness

Starting with what you checked in the Acts of Kindness Planner, make a list below of 10 acts of kindness you would like to try for someone you already know and then also make a list of 10 acts of kindness you would like to try to a stranger.

The Top Ten to Try for Someone I Know:

1. ______________________________

2. ______________________________

3. ______________________________

4. ______________________________

5. ______________________________

6. ______________________________

7. ______________________________

8. ____________________

9. ____________________

10. ____________________

The Top Ten to Try for a Stranger:

1. ____________________

2. ____________________

3. ____________________

4. ____________________

5. ____________________

6. ____________________

7. ____________________

8. ____________________

9. ____________________

10. ____________________

5. Doing a Kind Act for Someone You Know

Perform one kind act that you identified for someone you know and answer the following questions. Try to choose something that you haven't done before.

Who did you do the kind act for and what did you do?

____

How did the person (or persons) you did kind act for respond and how did doing the kind act and their response make you feel?

Chapter 16

Community Positive Psychology

Be the change you wish to see in the world.
— Mahatma Gandhi

The focus of the lesson for this chapter is something we might call "community positive psychology." Psychology sometimes gets stuck in only focusing on individuals, as if we were completely isolated from our social network and the world around us. There is an area of psychology called "community psychology" that focuses on the effects of the broader community on the behavior of individuals and the effects of individuals on the community.

In this chapter and the next, we are going to make the bridge from individual to community well-being because the health of the community and how we participate in it strongly affects our individual happiness and well-being. In fact, it may be that most of what brings us happiness is rooted in and related to our place in the larger community and world.

If anything is the foundation for our connection with others, it is our capacity for empathy. Empathy may be what enables us to connect with others and what can make it difficult for us to be truly happy when those around us are suffering. In the earlier chapter on social intelligence, you learned about how our brains have mirror neurons that fire the same way when we see someone else do something as when we do the same thing. In fact, one of the neuroscientists who has studied them, Vilayanur Ramachandran, has called them "Gandhi neurons" because of how they connect us with each other.

The psychologist Paul Wong has identified different kinds of empathy that involve these mirror neurons and other aspects of our biology, such as oxytocin, the hormone involved in social bonding. Here are the five kinds of empathy that Wong has identified:

First, he says we have an "instinctual empathy" that is hardwired, we share with other species, and you see when animals of one species respond to the distress calls of another.

Second, we often experience "relational empathy" that refers to the stronger feeling of empathy we have for those we are in a close relationship with, know well, or care about.

Third, there is the "experiential empathy" that we have for those we share a common experience with, such as being depressed or having been abused or assaulted. It could also involve sharing a good experience, such as when people in a city celebrate together when their home team wins a championship.

Fourth, there is what Wong calls "basic empathy" that involves learning a set of skills such as when a counselor or therapist learns how to do active listening and pay more attention to non-verbal cues.

Finally, there is "advanced empathy" that involves a detective-like Sherlock Holmes ability to make clever inferences and put together seemingly trivial and unrelated clues to better understand another person. You might experience this with a good friend or counselor when they say something about you that makes you feel like they know you better than you know yourself.

The bottom line is that we not only have a hardwired, inborn capacity for empathy with humans and other living beings; we also often have stronger empathy for those we are close to and who have similar experiences. And finally, we can do much to train ourselves and learn ways to increase our empathy and extend it to the larger community.

One example where I saw this happen was with my wife who grew up not having any experience with dogs. When she first began living with our playful and affectionate German Shorthaired Pointer, she was surprised to find that this dog seemed to have very real feelings and even seemed to have the empathy to comfort her when she was upset.

Another powerful example of our capacity to grow in empathy is provided by Steven Pinker who reviewed the incidence of human violence over the past several hundred years and concluded that it was generally on the decline. Using the phrase coined by Abraham Lincoln, he titled the book *The Better Angels of Our Nature: Why Violence is on the Decline.* Pinker thinks that one of the main reasons that violence has declined is that our capacity to empathize was extended by the great increase in literacy, which made it possible for us to read about and thereby understand the lives and experiences of many more people.

If this has been the case for reading, then it may be much more so now because so many people can connect in real time around the world using computers, smart phones, and social media platforms. Of course, social media can also have a dark side that capitalizes on our tendency to categorize people as us vs. them or as being in the in-group or the out-group. This evolutionary tendency is similar to our negativity bias that focuses on apparent threats while missing many of the good things around us. Just as we evolved to pay so much attention to those threats, we may have also evolved to first mistrust those who seem strange or different to us.

But Pinker thinks that "the better angels of our nature" – through empathy – have been growing stronger. When we think about the implications of positive psychology for our life together, extending our capacity for empathy to ever larger circles may be a promising direction and challenge for the future. The special video you will watch for this chapter called the "empathetic civilization" is by the social theorist Jeremy Rifkin and may give you a better idea of what Pinker is saying and where positive psychology may enable us to go.

In light of Pinker's and Rifkin's work and the findings about the central importance of empathy, one of the most important choices that the positive psychology community may have to make is how much to focus on solely helping individuals become their best in competition with each other versus focusing on building healthy institutions and communities. So often psychology has mirrored the Western world and focused on helping individuals assumed to be competing in a zero-sum game with only winners or losers.

Not long ago, I went to a conference in California honoring the career of one of the co-founders of positive psychology as he was retiring – Mihaly Csikszentmihalyi. He was in his early 80s and despite a long and fruitful career studying things like creativity and flow, many people spoke about how he never forgot about the social, economic, and political repression that he, his family, and others suffered when he grew up in Eastern Europe.

After his final talk near the end of the conference, the first person who raised his hand asked him what he wanted his legacy to be and what his hopes were for the future of positive psychology. Csikszentmihalyi said that as much as he knew that things like creativity and flow could make individuals successful, more than anything else he hoped that people would use what he discovered about creativity and flow to make ours a "win-win" world for everyone.

I think this may be one of the most important lessons we are learning from positive psychology about our relationship with the larger community. Because of our capacity for empathy and how important relationships, engagement, and meaning are to us, we may not really be happy unless we become our best as individuals and also work to bring out the best in the people and communities around us.

Workbook Tasks for the Chapter

The tasks for today are designed to help you think about and experience what we are discovering about how to create a better life together:

First, as after every chapter, there is a link to a video where you can see and hear me going over the lesson for this chapter.

Second, there is a special video called the "Empathetic Civilisation" by Jeremy Rifkin for you to watch and then reflect on the experiences that you may have had that enabled you to extend your empathy beyond your immediate family and social network. This video presents one of the most compelling visions of what a "community positive psychology" might have as a goal for increasing the happiness of all of us in the future.

Third, there is a task that involves doing one of the kind acts for a stranger from the top 10 list you created in the last chapter and answering questions about what you did and how it may have affected you and the other people involved. Doing kind acts both for people you know and don't know will help you understand how their effects on you may be similar and different and how they may both be important in unique ways.

Fourth, the next task involves making a list of the groups of people or communities that you are most grateful for and writing something about why you are grateful for them. This will help you understand how important these larger groups and communities may be to us in addition to other individual people and our smaller circle of friends and family members.

Fifth, there is a task that begins with making a list of the causes or things that you could be involved with that might have a positive impact on the larger world. There is also a place where you can rate their potential importance and your willingness and ability to do something to support one or more of them. This task may help you find new causes that you may value and enjoy being involved and finding ways to use your strengths to support.

1. Author's Video for this Lesson

Here is the link for the video of me going over the lesson for this chapter.

https://youtu.be/7nDAjP5Jf2g

2. Special Video – "RSA Animate: The Empathetic Civilisation"

Watch the video and reflect on what experiences you have had that have enabled you to extend your empathy to people who are different from you in some way such as gender, ethnicity, sexual orientation, language, culture, etc.

https://www.youtube.com/watch?v=l7AWnfFRc7g

3. Kind Act for a Stranger

Perform one of the kind acts you identified in the last chapter you would like to try for a stranger and answer the following questions. Try to do something you haven't done before.

Who did you do the kind act for and what did you do?

____

____

____

____

____

How did the person (or persons) that you did the kind act for respond and how did the whole experience make you feel?

____

____

____

____

____

How was the effect on you of doing a kind act for a stranger similar to or different from the effect on you of doing a kind act for someone you know, as was a task in the last chapter?

4. Gratitude for Groups and Communities

Make a list of the groups of people or communities that you are most grateful for and write down something that you are grateful to each of them for.

5. Community Cause Inventory

Using the "Community Cause Inventory" (see Appendix J), list the causes that are important and rate their potential importance and your willingness and ability to be involved in each of them.

What cause would you most like to support? What could you do to support it?

Chapter 17

Fairness and Justice

Injustice anywhere is a threat to justice everywhere.
— Martin Luther King, Jr.

In the last chapter, you learned about how much the larger community may affect our happiness as individuals and that being happy and having a life worth living may mean working to improve that community. In this chapter, the lesson is about what may help to guide us in making the difficult moral choices that we may need to make along the way.

We all have a sense of fairness that evolved to enable us to live with and get along with other people. In the special video for this chapter, you will see how this sense of fairness may even exist in other species or animals. This sense of fairness readily becomes apparent when you see one sibling in a family get more dessert than another or when someone cuts in front of you in line at the grocery store.

In order to get along with each other and have a just and healthy society, it is important that things be distributed fairly, and that there is justice for those who are harmed or who harm others. The author Karen Armstrong has pointed out that every world religion has a version of the Golden Rule, which in its Christian form, is to "do unto others as you would have them do unto you." At the same time, there is much debate about the concept of fairness and whether everyone should be treated the same or whether the justice system should take individual differences into account and focus more on equity in creating a level playing field for everyone.

In this chapter, I will tell you about three things that can benefit us in making the difficult moral choices that are sometimes necessary for living well together in community. The first two have to do with how we make these choices and the last may help us reduce the bias that can prevent us from making the best choice. There are two primary schools of thought about what may inform moral choices and they mirror the way that we sometimes feel pulled between our thoughts and emotions, on one hand, and between equality as treating everyone the same and equity as considering individual differences and the context.

The first school is called the Justice Tradition and was founded by Lawrence Kohlberg who identified six stages that we may move through from lower to higher levels of moral development.

The first stage is called "obedience and punishment driven" where we focus on the consequences of an action in deciding whether it is right or not. It is right as long as we don't get punished, which may simply mean not getting caught.

The second stage is called "self-interest driven" or the "what's in it for me stage" and it involves rationalizing that what we do is right as long as it is good for us as individuals.

The third stage is driven by "interpersonal accord and conformity" where we think that something we do is right as long as our close circle of family and friends approve or benefit.

The fourth stage is driven by "authority and social order obedience" where we obey the laws of the society because we don't think it could function if we didn't.

The fifth stage is driven by the "social contract" where laws are not viewed as set in stone but as social contracts than can be changed when a new law may do a better job of promoting the greater good.

Finally, the sixth stage is driven by universal ethical principles that are based on abstract reasoning about what may be moral or just across situations, cultures, and time.

From Kohlberg's perspective, it was rare to find anyone whose level of moral judgement consistently operated at the sixth stage. Also, you can see how the later stages place a greater emphasis on larger groups of people and making decisions that focus less on only one person or group vs. another. Thus, Kohlberg emphasized identifying the guiding principles for making moral choices and applying them equally and consistently across different people and situations.

Interestingly, the other primary school of thought that contrasts with Kohlberg's emphasis on abstract reason and universal principles was founded by one of his students. This student was Carol Gilligan, a woman who has focused more on the value of emotion, relationships, and context in making tough moral choices. She founded what has been called the Care Tradition of moral reasoning, which has three primary stages that may better reflect the experience of women and others who aren't part of a dominant power structure:

The first stage is called "orientation to individual survival" and it is focused on enabling us to make it through the earlier times in life when we are most helpless and vulnerable.

The second stage is called "goodness defined as self-sacrifice for others" and reflects the experience of women and others whose life may be defined by a role of service to others.

The third and final stage is called the "morality of non-violence: not hurting self or others" which echoes the philosophy of Gandhi and Martin Luther King, Jr. and stresses the self-kindness and self-compassion that we talked about in Chapter 8 about love.

In addition, because of the biases that may come with power, Gilligan places more emphasis on the context of those who are at a disadvantage and the necessity of considering their vulnerability. Thus, while Kohlberg emphasized universal principles that don't favor one group over another, Gilligan provides a potential corrective in asking us to also consider the context of those with less power.

The final thing that may help us make tough moral choices has to do with the way that the strength of Open-mindedness has been defined and understood in the VIA classification. While some define open-mindedness as simply being open to different people and perspectives, the VIA classification has defined it in a way that also takes into account common human biases. In the VIA classification, Open-mindedness is defined as actively searching for evidence against our favored beliefs, plans, or goals, and weighing such evidence fairly.

This active searching is necessary because of our "selective exposure" bias whereby we often unknowingly only expose ourselves to beliefs we are already comfortable and familiar with. Thus, a conservative person may only watch Fox news, a progressive person may only watch Rachel Maddow, and the empathy that a community positive psychology might try to foster and extend is cut short.

Selective exposure is similar to what has been called a "confirmation bias," which is the tendency to interpret new evidence as confirmation of our pre-existing beliefs. Thus, if a conservative person does watch Rachel Maddow or a progressive person watches Fox news, they may unknowingly maintain their beliefs by filtering what they hear through a particular way of interpreting it.

The result may be that people get lost in different narratives and become polarized losing out on the opportunity to make better moral decisions because they don't have the whole picture. The genius of the VIA definition of open-mindedness is that it emphasizes "actively searching for evidence against our favored beliefs" which can help us overcome our selective exposure and confirmation biases.

So, in putting together what we know about the need for making moral choices and what can help us make better ones, there are three important points to remember:

First, when we know that being happy and having a life worth living may involve working for a better community, we will be faced with tough choices about the kind of fairness and justice that are necessary for us to live well together.

Second, while Kohlberg demonstrated that universal ethical principles may help us avoid favoring one person, situation, or group over another; Gilligan challenged us to also take into account the way that having power may distort the picture and create a bias against those who are most vulnerable.

Third, the kind of open-mindedness that actively searches for evidence contradicting what we assume to be true may help us avoid the kind of biases that Gilligan highlights and that people in a dominant group or with power may be particularly vulnerable to.

Workbook Tasks for the Chapter

The tasks focus on our relationship with the community and how to foster fairness and justice in our relationships with each other and the larger community and world.

First, as after every chapter, there is a link to a video where you can see and hear me going over the lesson for this chapter.

Second, there is a special video to watch about a fascinating experiment about fairness with Capuchin monkeys and a question for you to reflect on regarding when you may have had a similar reaction as the monkey who was treated unfairly.

Third, there is a task that involves writing about ways you may have fallen into selective exposure and how you can practice open-mindedness to reduce it. This may be a promising way for us to do our part in reducing polarization about things like religion and politics.

Fourth, the next task involves doing something to support one of the causes that you identified in the last chapter and writing about what you did and how it went. This can help us understand the meaning and gratification we can find in contributing to the greater good.

Fifth, we want you to identify ways that you can demonstrate love, kindness, and compassion for yourself and do at least one of them in the near future. One of the reasons that people are not able to sustain acts of kindness and support for the causes that they believe in is that they do not take adequate care of themselves. As we discussed in the chapter on love, the ability to love and be kind and compassionate to your self is a form of love that can be very important but that many of us may neglect or don't practice well.

1. Author Video for this Lesson

Here is the link for the video of me going over the lesson for this chapter.

https://youtu.be/YO4QaE4Dxmk

2. Special Video - "Two Monkeys Were Paid Unequally"

Watch the video and reflect on where you have had a similar reaction to being treated unfairly. What feelings did you have and what were you motivated to do?

https://www.youtube.com/watch?v=meiU6TxysCg

3. Countering Selective Exposure with Open-mindedness

Write about the ways that you think you have fallen into selective exposure and how you might be able to use open-mindedness, as defined in the VIA classification, to reduce it.

____

____

____

____

____

____

4. Do Something to Support a Cause

Begin by reviewing the list of the causes you would like to support and what you wrote for your action plan if you did the Community Cause Inventory task in the last chapter. Next, select a cause that you rated highly in terms of importance and your willingness and ability to support it. Finally, do something to actually support the cause that you have chosen and answer the questions below.

What cause did you contribute to and what did you do?

How did what you do affect the other people involved? How did it affect you?

How was the effect on you of doing something to support a cause similar to or different from the effect on you of doing the acts of kindness you may have done in the previous two chapters for a stranger and for someone you knew?

5. Self-Love

There are two steps to the activity. First, brainstorm about the ways that you could demonstrate love, kindness, and/or compassion toward yourself and then do one of them and write about how it affected you.

What are five things that you could do to demonstrate love, kindness, and/or compassion toward yourself in the next week or two? Which would you most like to try and can plan to do in the next week or two?

____

____

____

____

____

____

What did you to expressed self-love for yourself and how did it go? What did you learn about how you can better love yourself in the future?

____

____

____

____

____

____

____

Chapter 18

Forgiveness

Unforgiveness is like drinking poison yourself and waiting for the other person to die.

— Marianne Williamson

Welcome to the final chapter of the third part of the positive psychology challenge!

First, I want to thank you for staying with it during this part. If you were used to other kinds of psychology, you may not have expected such a strong emphasis on your relationships with others and the larger community and world.

Second, I want to warn you that the focus of this lesson may not be for the faint of heart and also may not be something you are struggling with right now. But it is something that represents one of the best hopes that we have for healing the wounds we sometimes inflict on each other and for halting the cycle of violence and suffering we can become trapped in. That something is forgiveness.

It was only recently that someone in psychology was finally bold enough to attempt to study it. The person most responsible for bringing the study of forgiveness to the forefront in psychology is Everett Worthington – after his mother was murdered in 1996! The emotional fallout of the murder was so devastating to him and his family that it resulted in his brother committing suicide.

So, Everett didn't study forgiveness out of a casual interest, but because he was desperately trying to find a way to do it himself and didn't know how. He ended up publishing several papers and writing a couple of excellent books about it. Eventually, he and his sister were able to forgive and find the peace that they sought. Now, more than two decades later, there is a rich and growing body of research and theory on forgiveness and on what we can do to foster it in our lives

Probably the best place to start is to be clear about what we mean by forgiveness. Just what is it? It turns out that people have lots of different definitions and perspectives on forgiveness and that some of them may be more damaging and destructive than helpful. Robert Enright is another psychologist who has written a book about forgiveness and he helps us understand what forgiveness is by first telling us what it is not.

One, forgiveness is not excusing or pardoning what another person has done.

Two, it is not trying to justify or rationalize that it was okay for them to do it.

Three, forgiveness does not mean denying the harm of what someone has done.

Four, and this is a big one, forgiveness does not mean having to forget what another person did to hurt us. We may eventually forget it, but as George Santayana said, "those who cannot remember the past are condemned to repeat it." It may be important for us to remember so that we can protect ourselves and not allow others to hurt us in the same way.

Fifth, and this is also a big one for some of us, forgiveness does not necessarily mean getting back together or continuing to be in a relationship with someone who hurt us. We may choose to if they change their behavior – but we can forgive someone for what they have done to us even if it is better not to go back to them.

If these are some things that forgiveness is not, then what it is? First, forgiveness is giving up or ceasing to harbor resentment for a wrong that another has committed against us. This doesn't mean it is easy or happens overnight. Forgiveness usually takes time and it may be the greater the harm, the more time we will need to work through it.

Second, forgiveness involves reducing the negative feelings, thoughts, and behaviors we have toward the person who hurt us. When we are close to the time someone has hurt us, this may not seem possible but is likely to change with patience and self-compassion.

Third, if we have been in a relationship for a long time with the person who hurt us, we may again begin to have some good feelings about them, whether or not they change their behavior and whether or not we decide to continue a relationship with them

Fourth, and this is probably the most important, forgiveness is a process that can take a lot of time and mental and physical energy. It can be exhausting to continue to experience the intensity of feelings and the ups and downs that we may experience along the way.

Fifth, forgiveness often eventually seems like a paradox. While we thought we would be diminished and never escape the anger, hurt, or preoccupation with what happened – one day we actually feel lighter, enriched, and free in a way we didn't think possible!

So, on the one hand, forgiveness is not excusing, pardoning, justifying, denying, or trying to forget what someone has done to us and we do not necessarily need to go back or continue a relationship with the person who hurt us.

On the other hand, forgiveness is a process that can set us free in ways we may not have thought possible. We may become free from the anger, pain, and preoccupation with what was done to us. In its place, we may be pleasantly surprised with the kindness, love, and compassion we feel for ourselves and others – and even for the person who hurt us.

Some of the most encouraging good news that positive psychology has brought to us is that forgiveness is possible. But before we finish this chapter, I want to say something about the kind of things that people like Everett Worthington and Robert Enright have suggested might help make it more possible for us to forgive.

The first is to commit ourselves to the process even though it may take time and sometimes it may not seem like we are making much progress.

The second is to freely express our thoughts and feelings about what happened in writing, with the goal of eventually being able to write about our intention to forgive.

The third is to get the support of other people with at least one person we can really trust to confide in and who understands how forgiveness can be a long process.

The fourth is to practice self-compassion in being patient and kind with ourselves and to forgive ourselves when we feel like giving up or don't think we are making progress. Sometimes the first step in forgiveness is to forgive ourselves for feeling stuck for so long and not wanting to forgive.

The fifth is to try to develop empathy and understanding for how someone could do what they did to hurt us - and for how we may sometimes do things that hurt others.

The sixth thing that may help us with forgiveness is to be open to the possibility of the stress-related growth that we talked about, where we learn or benefit from what happened in some way that is good for us. Examples might include learning to have more love and compassion for ourselves or increased wisdom in knowing how not to get hurt again.

There is one final thing that Everett Worthington, Robert Enright, and others who have studied forgiveness think is particularly valuable. Once we feel like we have gotten the freedom and peace we sought in forgiving, many find it useful to do something to mark, celebrate, or savor what they have accomplished. This could include things like writing a forgiveness letter, releasing balloons, or having a party with the friends who were with us along the way to celebrate our accomplishment with them.

In conclusion, while forgiveness may be hard to practice, it offers great hope for healing the many ways we hurt each other. It is reported that Gandhi said, "An eye for an eye leaves the whole world blind." If so, then forgiveness may be what makes it possible for us to see again and find our way out the cycles of violence in which we sometimes get stuck.

This third part of the challenge has been about what we can do to better create the kinds of relationships and communities that we need in order to be truly happy. When we inevitably get off track in doing things that either unintentionally or intentionally hurt each other, forgiveness may be a bridge that offers us the hope of getting back on the track of creating a society that enables all of us to thrive and make the most of our lives together.

Now that we have nearly come to the end of this part of this challenge, I hope you will take time to savor what you have done so far and look forward to the positive vision of the future that you can create during the fourth and final part of this challenge.

Workbook Tasks for the Chapter

Here are the tasks which are designed to help you better understand and foster forgiveness for others and for yourself:

First, as after every chapter, there is a link to a video where you can see and hear me going over the lesson for this chapter.

Second, there is a special video to watch with an extraordinary example of the power of forgiveness where a mother is able to forgive the person who killed her son. When you watch this, try to forgive yourself if you feel like you could never do something like that. Then, just try to understand how she did it and what difference it made for her and the person that she forgave.

Third, there is a task that involves writing about a time when someone did something that hurt you. This includes focusing on the thoughts and feelings you experienced and the potential benefits you might experience in forgiving this person. Writing this way can help you decide whether you want to try to practice forgiveness and break the ice in doing it.

Fourth, there is also a task that involves writing about a time you failed or let yourself down which also includes focusing on the thoughts and feelings you experienced and what you can do to be kind and compassionate in forgiving yourself. Many think it is harder to forgive themselves than it is to forgive others and here is your chance to learn to do it.

Fifth, there are reflection questions about what surprised you the most in this third part of the challenge about your relationship with others and what you would most like to remember. These were included to enable you to better understand how your own happiness and well-being may be rooted in your relationships and the larger community.

1. Author's Video for this Lesson

Here is the link for the video of me going over the lesson for this chapter.

https://youtu.be/Ex5mrm2P8Pg

2. Special Video – "The power of forgiveness" with Steve Hartman

Watch the video and think about what made it possible for the mother to forgive the person who killed her son.

https://www.youtube.com/watch?v=o2BITY-3Mp4

3. A Time When You Were Hurt and Benefits of Forgiveness

Write about a time when someone did something that hurt you. Include the thoughts and feelings you experienced about it and the potential benefits to you in forgiving this person.

____

____

____

____

____

4. Forgiving Yourself for Something

Write about a time when you feel like you failed or let yourself down. Include the thoughts and feelings you experienced about it, and what you can do to be kind and compassionate in forgiving yourself.

5. Reflection Questions

What surprised you the most in what you learned in this third part of the challenge?

What happened in this third part of the challenge that you most want to remember? How can you remember and make it more a part of your life in the future?

Part 4 – Creating the Best Possible Future

What is this part about?

Purpose: The purpose of this part is to enable you to develop a plan for best using what you have learned in this challenge to create the best possible life you can imagine.

Topics: There are chapters about fostering the optimism, hope, humor, appreciation, gratitude, and sense of meaning and purpose that will help you in making this happen.

Activities: The most important activities focus on imagining your best possible life and charting your course by creating a map with a step-by-step plan that can enable you to achieve it and make it a reality.

Chapter 19

Creating a Better Future

Set a goal so big that you can't achieve it
until you grow into the person who can.
— Zig Ziglar

Welcome to the fourth and final part of this positive psychology challenge!

This focus for this part is on putting what you have been learning and doing into a plan for a better future. From the start, this challenge has been about using positive psychology to increase your happiness and well-being and making the most of your life.

The first part was basic training to help you identify what would make you most happy, learn about the ways that psychology can help you achieve it, and build a foundation in mindfulness, resilience, and the wisdom and creativity you need to find your way.

The second part focused on discovering the best in yourself, identifying your strengths, and learning about what would enable you to use them to achieve your goals. This included learning about authenticity, perseverance, courage, self-efficacy, and self-control.

The third part of the challenge enabled you to improve your relationships and have a positive impact on the larger community and world around you by learning about social intelligence, kindness, love, the value of community, fairness, and forgiveness.

The activities and videos reflected this progression with the primary exercises focused on seeing more of the good around you in the first part, using more of the best within yourself in the second, and improving your relationships with others and the world in the third.

The primary exercises for this last part will involve creating a vision of the best possible life for yourself in the future and creating a plan for using what you have been learning and doing in this challenge to make it happen.

In addition to this first lesson that will get your started in this process, the lessons for this last part focus on the VIA strengths in the category of transcendence. These strengths enable us to transcend or go beyond our previous way of life and make the most of our life and live it to the fullest.

Here are the strengths we will cover to help you do this:

1. Optimism and Hope - the strengths that may help you the most in bringing about a better future.
2. Humor – the strength that can enable you to smile or laugh in almost any situation or circumstance along the way.

3. Appreciation and Gratitude – strengths that can make so much of our lives precious regardless of the challenges we are facing or the stress we are experiencing.
4. Meaning and Purpose – strengths that enable us to focus on what is most important and what may do the most to make our lives worth living.

The final chapter will be a review and celebration of everything that you have learned and done as a part of this challenge.

With this in mind, I'll now turn to the main focus of the lesson for this chapter: the creative process that will help you design a pathway to a better future. This process is called the PATH process. PATH is an acronym that stands for Planning Alternative Tomorrows with Hope and it is a planning process developed by Jack Pearpoint, John O'Brien, and Marsha Forrest. The PATH process provides a series of steps that we can take to make positive change happen.

There are eight steps in the PATH process and there will be a task for the first four chapters of this final part that will involve completing part of this process. You will do two of the eight steps in each of the first four chapters. In this chapter, I'll give you an introduction to the process and briefly walk you through the eight steps. In order to provide additional information about the PATH process, we have included a special section in Appendix K titled "Guidelines for the PATH Process" which also has links for videos that will also help you understand the process.

So here we go. First, the PATH process uses a graphic approach that will help you visualize the steps it will take to achieve the kind of future that you want most. The process involves creating a map of these steps on a large sheet or sheets of poster board and writing down what will help you reach your goals. Thus, the first thing we will ask you to do is to get two pieces of white poster board that are each approximately 2 by 3 feet that you can tape together to create one continuous poster board that is approximately 2 by 6 feet. If you don't have enough space, you can tape the two sheets of poster board together so they fold in half for easier storage. You will also need to get a set of medium-point colored Sharpies or other colored writing utensils you can use to write on the poster board or paper.

It is also possible to create a visual representation of your PATH on paper that rolls up or is created with computer software such as PowerPoint. Most people prefer to do it on a large poster board because they can put it up where they can see it and it is stronger and will last longer than paper that is much thinner. Several of my students have told me how glad they were that they didn't use computer software because they liked to be able to touch it and use their hands to do the writing and any drawing that may be involved. By the way, you do not have to be an artist or good at drawing to do this. I have seen some great PATH posters with minimal drawing and mostly words or lines using different colors.

After you have the materials that you need, you will be ready to begin the first of the eight steps of the PATH process. The first step is called Touching the Dream and involves envisioning a "north star" that represents your dream of what you would like and could have if there weren't any limits. This "north star" will orient and guide you during the rest of the process and will be the starting point for breaking your dream down into achievable goals. This is probably the step where drawing something or having a simple visual image, symbol, or picture may be most useful. Sometimes being able to visualize something you want in the future might enable you to discover things that may be harder to find or articulate using words alone. For example, if you want to be successful in a sport, you might draw or use a picture of an Olympic medal or a trophy. If you are retired and would like to spend more time with your grandchildren, you might draw a house where you could always be with them and something that represents who they are or what they love to do.

The second step is called Sensing the Goal and involves identifying "positive and possible" goals for the future and a timeframe for reaching these goals. If you had a dream of increasing meaning in your life by helping troubled adolescents, for example, this step might involve setting the more specific goal of establishing a non-profit organization to help them. This is also where something like a gold medal representing your dream might get translated into a more specific goal you can work towards like winning or earning a medal at the marathon for your age group in the city where you live. For the dream of spending time with your grandchildren, you could write down a goal of moving to the same town where they live, giving them special gifts, or taking them on a trip that you might both enjoy.

While the first two steps are focused on the best possible future, the third step is called Ground in the Now and involves identifying where you are now in relation to reaching your goals. This may draw on what you learned about how mindfulness can enable us to change by first accepting where we are. The fourth step is called Invite Enrollment and involves identifying and inviting people who are in a good position to support and help you reach your goals. The PATH process calls this group of people your "dream team" and this step will draw on what you learned in the last part of this challenge about improving your relationships with others.

The fifth step is called Building Strength and involves recognizing ways to use your top strengths and build and use the other strengths and skills that you may need. This step will directly draw on much of what you learned about identifying and using strengths in the second part of this challenge. The final three steps involve making a plan to bridge the gap between now and achieving the vision you showed and described in the first two steps. The goals identified in these steps should follow the SMART acronym in that they are: (1) Specific, (2) Measurable, (3) Achievable, (4) Relevant, and (5) Time-bound.

The sixth step is to Identify Bold Steps for achieving your longer-term goals by setting shorter-term goals, the seventh step is Organizing the Month's Work by being specific about what you will do in the next month, and the eighth step is Committing to the First Step which means identifying and doing one thing now to get you started.

Because the PATH process may be new to you, I strongly recommend following the Guidelines for the PATH Process in Appendix K where is there a diagram that shows you where to put these steps on your poster. There are also links to three videos included with the guidelines and under the last task for this chapter. These videos may be the best way for you to see what a PATH poster can look like and what you may want to aim for.

Workbook Tasks for the Chapter

The tasks include getting started with the PATH process and creating a vision of your best possible life in the future.

First, as after every chapter, there is a link to a video where you can see and hear me going over the lesson for this chapter.

Second, there is a special video about the reaction of a little girl to getting what it is that she wants more than anything else. This is shown as an example of the joy and gratitude that it possible for us to experience when we achieve goals that mean the most to us.

Third, to enable you to get started thinking more about your future, there is an activity that was developed in positive psychology which has been shown to increase optimism, hope, happiness, and the likelihood of reaching your goals. This activity involves writing about what you may imagine as you best possible life. To do this, you will be asked to think about your life in the future and imagine that everything has gone as well as it possibly could. You will be asked to answer questions about where you might be living, what work you might be doing, who you might be with, and how you might be giving back to others.

Fourth, as noted above, you will need to find or purchase the material you will need for your PATH poster you will be working on for the first four chapters of this final part of the challenge. As noted above, what generally works best is to get two pieces of white poster board that are approximately 2 by 3 feet that you can tape together on the back to create one continuous poster board that is approximately 2 by 6 feet. In addition, it may be best to have or get a set of medium-point colored Sharpies or other colored writing utensils that you can use to write on the poster board.

Fifth, the final task involves completing the first two steps of the PATH process that are called Touching the Dream and Sensing the Goal. These steps are described in the lesson above and in the Guidelines for the PATH Process in Appendix K.

Sixth, there are reflection questions about the people you might like to invite to be a part of your "dream team" to support you in the PATH process and about which of your goals for the future may be most important.

1. Author Video for this Lesson

Here is the link for the video of me going over the lesson for this chapter.

https://youtu.be/4DQaekZLyZs

2. Special Video – "Lily's Disneyland Surprise"

Watch the video and think about this as an example of what it might be like for you when you accomplish an important goal and make one of your dreams come true.

https://www.youtube.com/watch?v=OOpOhlGiRTM&t=67s

3. Writing about Your Best Possible Life

This is an exercise that involves writing about the "best possible life" you can imagine for yourself in the future. Begin by thinking about your life in the future and imagining that everything has gone as well as it possibly could. You have worked hard and succeeded at using your strengths and accomplishing your life goals and you have realized your dreams.

If you are younger, this may include things like getting married and having a family, beginning the kind of career you most want, or moving to live somewhere you always wanted to live. If you are older, this may involve making the most of your later years by doing something you always wanted to do, contributing to a cause that means a lot to you, or finding peace in growing old and focusing on the little things you can enjoy and are grateful for. If you in the middle part of your life, the life you want most may be a combination of these kind of things or something entirely different. The main thing is that what you write about is both (1) the best that you can imagine if you use what you have learned about in this challenge and (2) also something that is within the realm of possibility.

In writing about your best possible life, be as clear, specific, and detailed as possible. You can use the following questions as a guide if they are relevant for you and your life situation:

a. Where would you be living?

b. What kind of people would you be with?

c. What kind of work would you be doing?

d. What would you be doing for recreation and fun?

e. How might you be giving back to other people or the world beyond?

____

____

____

____

____

____

____

____

____

____

____

____

____

____

____

4. Getting Materials for the PATH Process

To begin the PATH process, you will need to get two pieces of white poster board that are approximately 2 by 3 feet that you can tape together on the back to create one continuous poster board that is approximately 2 by 6 feet. You will also need to get a set of medium-point colored Sharpies or other colored writing utensils that you can use to write on the poster board. You can find these at places like *Michael's* or *Hobby Lobby* but may also be able to find them as places liked *Walmart* or *Target*. If you don't have a lot of space, it may help to fold the two sheets of poster board that you tape together for easier storage.

5. Starting the PATH Process

Using your poster board and colored writing utensils and following the Guidelines for the PATH Process in Appendix K, complete the 1st and 2nd steps. The 1st step called Touching the Dream involves envisioning a "north star" that represents what you want most and would be the best you can imagine with no limits (e.g., "I'd like to be the next Albert Einstein or Maya Angelou"). The 2nd step called Sensing the Goal involves identifying "positive and possible" future goals (e.g., "I'd like to be an excellent scientist like Albert Einstein" or a respected poet and social activist like Maya Angelou.") and a realistic time frame for reaching them (e.g., 3-6 years for becoming an excellent scientist or poet).

Before you get started, be sure to watch the following videos to help you better understand the process and what the finished product might look like. They were produced by North Star Facilitators, the Spectrum Society for Community Living, and our own Center for Applied Positive Psychology with Tanya Kallan, John Freisinger, and Paul Smith:

https://northstarfacilitators.com/the-path-process

https://www.youtube.com/watch?v=_ecv_VN9KyI

https://www.youtube.com/watch?v=LlKACFFEUdc

Chapter 20

Optimism and Hope

Hope lies in dreams, in imagination, and in the courage of those who dare to make dreams into reality.

— Jonas Salk

In this chapter, you are going to learn about the strengths that may be the most important for creating a better future: optimism and hope. In the last chapter, one of your tasks was to write about your best possible life. This is one of the go-to activities developed in positive psychology that people have found especially useful for increasing optimism and hope.

You have also started the PATH process, which began with a focus on the future in the first two steps. These involved touching your dream and sensing your most important long-term goals. This kind of looking forward to a better future and beginning to see how it is possible is what optimism and hope are all about.

While optimism and hope have been defined in several different ways, psychology has tried to define them in specific ways to make it possible to study them. In psychology, optimism is defined as generally expecting more good things than bad to happen in the future. In addition, while hope has sometimes been associated with something that may be false or unrealistic, in psychology it has been defined in a realistic and practical way that has to do with being able to reach our future goals.

The person who wrote the first textbook about positive psychology spent most of his career focusing on this kind of hope. His name is Rick Snyder and he defined hope in a way that uses the words of a saying that is probably familiar to most of you: "Where there is a will, there is a way!" In Snyder's view of hope, there are two things that make a better future possible. The first is the "will" to make it happen and the second is a "way" or several ways to make it happen. So, hope is having both the will and the way to reach your goals for a better future.

This "will" and this "way" draw on some things that you have already learned about. The "will" to make it happen involves both the grit and the self-efficacy we covered during the second part of the challenge. You may remember that grit is perseverance plus having a purpose you are passionate about and that self-efficacy is the belief that you can do what it takes to reach a goal or fulfill that purpose. The "way" or ways of hope draw on the wisdom and creativity that you learned about at the end of the first part of this challenge. You may remember that wisdom is the practical knowledge we need for everyday life and creativity involves finding new ways to do something that is useful or beneficial for us.

In order to make hope happen and achieve what we hope for, we need to have a goal or purpose we want to achieve like what you envisioned in the best possible life activity and did for the first two steps of the PATH process. Once you have a goal or purpose that you are passionate about, you can work on increasing your will to create the pathways to it. In addition to having that consistent goal, the other thing you can do is simply to persevere, to just keep taking that next single step, which will also increase your self-efficacy.

Let's say that a goal you are passionate about is to become a black belt in karate. The single step that begins this long journey might be looking for a beginner's class that you can take. But let's say that you aren't able to find a karate class after a week of exercising your perseverance in looking through the local newspaper. This is where the "way" part comes into play and where exercising wisdom and creativity, along with a dose of self-efficacy, may help. For example, in the wisdom that comes from your personal experience, you remember that you have an old friend who took a karate classes a couple years ago.

You contact her and get the phone number of her old instructor who is currently not teaching but who happens to know three other instructors that you can contact. So you are on your way to finding the class you need to start with. At this and every step of the way – especially when you are facing the biggest challenges – like the first test for your first belt – you may need to exercise and build two strengths we talked about. You may need to increase your belief that you can do it – what we called "self-efficacy" - as well as the discipline or self-control that it may take to practice. In Chapters 11 and 12 you learned about several proven ways to increase each.

The problem that many people have in trying to use optimism and hope to reach their goals is that they often leave out that "way" part or what they need to do to get there. There is a common view about positive thinking that equates it with the kind of magical thinking that says if we only think about something it will suddenly appear in our driveway. One reason people may like to think about it this way is that if it is true, they won't have to do a lot of work! It may also be that when we see someone else get something we know they have been thinking about, we may assume they got it just by thinking about it and don't realize how much they may have actually done to work for it.

There was a study conducted by the psychologist Shelley Taylor that sheds light on this problem. She randomly assigned college students who were going to take a big test to two different groups. The first group was asked to imagine themselves getting back a big test with an A on it and the second group was asked to imagine doing what they thought it might take for them to get an A on the test. The second group not only did better on the test and got more As, they also spent more time studying and the time that they spent studying was strongly related to how well they did on the test.

During the first part of this challenge you were asked to write down three good things that happened during the day as one of the tasks for many of the chapters. While this may not have always directly caused more good things to happen around you, just being aware and looking for them probably made it more likely you would find some of them and eventually do things to make some of them happen more often in the future. Similarly, thinking about getting an A on a test might not directly cause you to do better, but it may make it more likely by increasing your motivation to study.

This is how it may be with writing about your best possible life and envisioning a better future in first steps of the PATH process. This may increase your motivation and belief that you may get there. But the way to really make Snyder's kind of hope happen is to use that motivation to begin to create the path you need to get there, and then of course to carry it out. That is what the rest of this challenge is all about.

Workbook Tasks for the Chapter

Here are tasks to enable you to increase and benefit more from optimism and hope:

First, as after every chapter, there is a link to a video where you can see and hear me going over the lesson for this chapter.

Second, there is a special video about a young boy who does something that he always wanted to do and his whole community celebrates with him. This an example of what is possible when we continue to work towards our most important goals even when they may sometimes seem out of reach.

Third, the next task is to complete the 3rd and 4th steps of the PATH process as described in Appendix K Guidelines for the PATH Process and in the videos that the appendix provides links for. The 3rd step is called Ground in the Now and involves identifying where you are now in relation to your long-term goals and the 4th step is called Invite Enrollment and involves inviting those you would like to have on your "dream team" to encourage and support you in working towards your goals and best possible life.

Fourth, this task is to do something to increase your pathways for "making hope happen" for you. It involves going back through this workbook and making a list of the lessons, exercises, videos, and questions that you think might most help you on your path to your best possible life. This will help you make the best use of what you have learned and done as a part of this challenge.

Fifth, there are reflection questions about what you can best use from what you have learned in this challenge, or anywhere else in your life, to enable you to achieve the goals for your best possible life. This will help you be more specific and go into more detail about what you can actually do to use what you have learned to reach your goals.

1. Author Video for this Lesson

Here is the link for the video of me going over the lesson for this chapter.

https://youtu.be/Dd1bvK5xPck

2. Special Video - "Wow: Autistic Waterboy scores Non-Stop 3-pointers!"

After you watch the video, think about what it might be like for you to celebrate reaching some of your most important goals with those who helped you achieve them.

https://www.youtube.com/watch?v=WV1akgvFknk

3. PATH Process Steps 3 and 4

The task is to complete the 3rd and 4th steps of the PATH process as described in the Guidelines for the PATH Process in Appendix K. The 3rd step is called Ground in the Now and involves identifying where you are now in relation to your goals and where you most want to be in the future. The 4th step is called Invite Enrollment and identifying and inviting the people you would like to have on your "dream team" to support you in the PATH process. In order to fully understand these steps and what to aim for, be sure to watch the videos that Appendix K provides the links for if you haven't already.

Who are the people who you would most like to have on your "dream team" and how do you think each can help, support, and encourage you on your PATH? After you invite them, put a check mark next to those that agree to be on your dream.

____

____

____

____

____

____

____

____

____

____

____

4. Making Hope Happen

The task is to do something to increase the "ways" for you to "make hope happen." This involves reviewing the lessons, videos, exercises, and questions so far in this challenge and listing those you think may be most helpful for achieving your best possible life.

If possible, it might be best to flip through each of the chapters, make notes as you go, and then highlight or rank those you think are most important. You might be surprised how much we can forget if we don't go back and review and rehearse what we have learned.

After you have completed your review and have a list of things you most want to use in achieving the kind of life you envision for yourself, write down the top 10 or so below along with notes about why each may be important and how you might use them.

____

____

____

____

____

____

____

____

____

____

____

____

____

5. Reflection Questions

Select 3-5 of the most important things that learned in this challenge and write about how you can use them to realize your best possible life.

If possible, identify anything else that you have learned in your life that you can use to help you reach your best possible life and write about how these things may help you.

Chapter 21

Humor

Humor can alter any situation and help us cope
at the very instant we are laughing.
— Allen Klein

Now we are going to talk about what makes us laugh. It may seem strange to have a lesson about humor at all, even more during the final part of this challenge where you are envisioning and creating a path to a best possible life. But that is part of the point about humor and why we need it so much.

Humor is about recognizing the incongruities of life, the things that don't seem to fit in the world around us, in our friends and family members, and especially in ourselves. When you think about the life you want for yourself in the future as you do for the "best possible life" activity in Chapter 19, you might be struck by how far away it may seem from the life you are living right now. Humor can help us laugh and make light of how much of a difference this can be and use it as a motivation for change rather than something to be discouraged about.

During the first part of this challenge, we talked about the power of positive reappraisal, which is our ability to think about things in a new way that brings out more of the best in ourselves and the world around us. Humor can work for us in a similar way and at times can be even more powerful.

There have been surveys asking people what qualities they think may be most important in a marriage partner where the answer has been humor, rather than intelligence or good looks. Even when you lose whatever good looks you had and get old enough to not be able to remember the last time you had an intelligent thought, you can still laugh and we often love those who make us laugh.

As with positive reappraisal, humor can shift our perspective in a way that can make us smile, laugh, and even feel joy in some of the worst of circumstances.

So, what is humor? It has been defined in at least three different ways.

First, and this may be what some of us are thinking about when we say we don't have a good sense of humor, it has been defined as the ability to make other people smile or laugh. The thing is that for some of us, we do this without even trying – or by accident when we are actually trying to be serious.

Second, humor has been defined as something close to the way I talked about it at the beginning of this lesson – as the playful recognition, enjoyment, or creation of incongruities.

This brings us back to what we may see in ourselves when, despite our highest aspirations, we make some of the same silly mistakes again and again.

Third, and this is where it can become a super power, humor has been defined as a cheerful view on adversity that allows us to see the lighter side of things and enables us to sustain a good mood – even when stress happens! This may be why in the VIA classification humor is listed under the category of transcendence. It may enable us to transcend or rise above our stressful circumstances.

The other thing that is wonderful about humor is that there are so many different forms. Like with our strengths and the things we love to do, it may be vital for us to discover what kinds of humor are our personal favorites. There may be some forms of humor that don't appeal to us at all, while there may be others that once we are exposed to them, we can't get enough of them.

Here is a sample of different kinds of humor. Think about which are your favorites.

The first one is a joke – seriously - which is a short story that ends with a funny, climactic twist… "What did the Buddhist say to the vendor at the hot dog stand?... Make me one with everything."

Another verbal form of humor that can be a form of a joke is a riddle - which is question that calls for a clever or unexpected answer… "What goes up but never goes down?... Your age." There are probably some of us that don't find that one very funny!

And then there is overstatement like when you say "I sure did great" on a test that you barely passed, or understatement like saying that "Phoenix, Arizona can get a little warm in the summer."

One form of humor made famous on the *Candid Camera* television show is the practical joke where you create a strange or unlikely situation for someone and then see how they react. There is a famous *Candid Camera* scene called The Power of Conformity where everyone on an elevator, except the unknowing target person, do strange things together with the unknowing target following right along. You will see this as your special video for this chapter because not only is it funny, it also shows the dangers of blind conformity.

Of course, there is also the kind of physical humor that the *Three Stooges* became famous for as they slapped and poked at each other with the same familiar sounds as if they were playing the drums or in a dance. Then there is the witty banter that Bud Abbott and Lou Costello made famous in their *Who's on First?* routine, where confusion reigns regarding the name of the players on a baseball team.

The final kind of humor I want to mention is satire or parody, which is used to make fun of the shortcomings of those who may take themselves too seriously. While this can be a form of hostile humor that can hurt it targets, it has also been effectively used to challenge abusive people in power who may be difficult to challenge otherwise. It also may be a unique and powerful tool to use with ourselves to keep us humble in accepting our personal flaws and imperfections.

The bottom line is that the power of humor is no joke, and that although it can sometimes be used to harm others, it may be one of the most powerful things we have to keep us smiling and sane on the most stressful and challenging parts of our path.

Since the dawn of positive psychology, there has been increasing research on the effects of humor showing that not only can it make us laugh, but that is also good for our health and well-being. One, it can help us recover more quickly from surgery and illness. Two, it can enable us to better deal with our mortality. Three, it can reduce some of the harmful aspects of the stress response. Four, it has been shown to improve immune function.

Finally, there are things that even the most humorless among us can do to increase the presence of humor and its benefits in our lives. The psychologist Paul McGhee has developed what he calls the *Seven Humor Habits* program, which has been shown to increase optimism, self-efficacy, and positive emotions while also decreasing anxiety, depression, and stress. You can 'google' him and the name of the program for the details about how to practice them, but here are the seven habits:

1. Surround yourself with humor.
2. Cultivate a playful attitude.
3. Laugh more often and more heartily.
4. Create your own verbal humor.
5. Look for humor in everyday life.
6. Take yourself lightly and laugh at yourself.
7. Find humor in the midst of stress.

So, when you are charting your course to your best possible life – humor might help you laugh at all the ways you may fall short and more quickly recover from set-backs. You might also find yourself laughing when you are surprised at how well you are doing and at all of the strange and unexpected things that are bound to happen along the way.

Believe it or not, science has finally confirmed what many of us have suspected all along. Humor can bring a smile to almost any situation and help us both have fun and make the most of our lives. Seriously!

Workbook Tasks for the Chapter

The following tasks are designed to help you continue to develop a plan for a better future and understand how you can use humor to enable you to achieve it.

First, as after every chapter, there is a link to a video where you can see and hear me going over the lesson for this chapter.

Second, the special video is a classic *Candid Camera* TV show scene filmed on an elevator about the power of conformity. This may help you appreciate humor and think about where you may have fallen into conformity and what you can do to avoid it.

Third, the task is to write about how you can use your top strengths and what you have learned and done in this challenge to achieve your best possible life. This will enable you to identify and describe specific ways you can use what you have learned and help you complete the 5th and 6th steps of the PATH process.

Fourth, the next task is to complete the 5rd and 6th steps of the PATH process as described in the Appendix K Guidelines for the PATH process. The 5th step is called Building Strength and involves identifying ways to use your top strengths and build and use other strengths and skills that you may need. The 6th step is called Identify Bold Steps and involves identifying your goals for reaching a middle point in meeting your long-term goals.

Fifth, there are reflection questions about the kind of humor that you enjoy the most and how you might use humor to help you achieve your goals and realize your best possible life. This will be you the chance to think about how you might use humor to deal with the stressful times and lows in your life and use it to celebrate your achievements and the highs.

1. Author Video for this Lesson

Here is the link for the video of me going over the lesson for this chapter.

https://youtu.be/XMB19WU8Wr4

2. Special Video – "Human Behaviour experiment Lift Antics"

Watch the video and reflect on where you have fallen into conformity. Think about how you may be able to prevent that and think and act in ways that are more true to you and the path that you want to take in your life.

https://www.youtube.com/watch?v=XZDLbbfT9_Q

Where have you fallen into the kind of conformity that you saw in the video? What can you to avoid it and act in ways that are true to who you are?

___

___

___

___

___

3. Using What You Learned to Realize Your Best Possible Life

Write about how you can use your top strengths and what you have learned and done in this challenge to achieve your best possible life and the goals in your PATH. If you did last chapter's activity where you make a list of what might help you the most from this challenge and the rest of your life, then write about how you can use the most important of those things. If you haven't done that, then it may be best to review the lessons, videos, and activities in this workbook and make a list now. Finally, you may want to go over the "340 Ways to Use Character Strengths" for ideas about using your strengths to reach your goals.

http://tayyabrashid.com/pdf/via_strengths.pdf

____

____

____

____

____

____

____

____

____

____

____

____

____

____

4. PATH Process Steps 5 and 6

This task is to complete the 5th and 6th steps of the PATH process as described in the Guidelines for the PATH Process in Appendix K. The 5th step is called Building Strength and involves listing your top strengths and how you can use them to reach your goals and listing the other strengths and skills you may need and how you can build and use them. The 6th step is called Identify Bold Steps and involves listing your goals for reaching a middle point in meeting the long-term goals that you identified in the 2nd stepIn order to fully understand these steps and what to aim for, be sure to watch the videos that Appendix K provides links for if you haven't already.

5. Reflection Questions

What kind of humor do you enjoy the most? Give specific examples if you can.

___

___

___

___

___

___

___

___

___

___

___

___

How can you use humor to help achieve your goals and realize your best possible life?

Chapter 22

Appreciation and Gratitude

I would maintain that thanks are the highest form of thought;
and that gratitude is happiness doubled by wonder.
— G.K. Chesterton

We are coming down the home stretch in this challenge. In the last chapter, we covered an often underrated strength that can bring a laugh or smile to almost any situation: humor.

In this chapter, we are going to talk about two other underrated strengths that can increase the value of almost anything in our lives – appreciation or what the VIA classification calls the Appreciation of Beauty and Excellence, and, simply put, Gratitude. While thinking about that best possible life that we are creating a path toward in the future, it is good to be able to know about and exercise these two strengths that can make every day of our lives precious.

We will begin with the Appreciation of Beauty and Excellence (or just "appreciation" as I often refer to it). To begin with, it may help to know that there are at least three main focuses for it.

1) The first focus is physical beauty, which we may most often see with our eyes. For me, it is the way the clouds paint the skies where I live in New Mexico, which for good reason is called the "Land of Enchantment." There may be only one Mona Lisa, but almost every day, especially around sunrise and sunset, the clouds glide and dance in an ever-changing pattern that even Leonardo Da Vinci couldn't completely capture. Physical beauty is something we may most associate with our richly endowed visual sense but we can also experience it through our other senses, as in the sound of music with that song we never tire of; the smells we love that help us feel peaceful and grounded; the taste of a gourmet meal; or the sensual pleasure we may experience while making love.

2) The second focus for appreciation is the excellence we see in exceptional displays of human skill or talent. The way that Michael Jordan played basketball transcended the sport and got people who never watched the game to tune in just to watch him. This kind of excellence can be one of the rewards for doing what you love, using your strengths, and having the experience of mastering something after months and years of practice. Yes, you appreciate the excellence of a Michael Jordan, who may have done one thing better than anyone else. But you can also appreciate excellence in overcoming obstacles that you saw in the boy with autism who sunk six three pointers in a row, or in Nick Vujicic, who with no arms and legs shows us how he has learned to do many things that we take for granted.

But it is the third focus of appreciation that may provide the best hope for humanity, especially when we view it in light of what we are learning about the biology of kindness and compassion. The third focus is acts of virtue, moral beauty, and goodness. When you witness the loving way that Mother Teresa embraced that dying person on the streets of Calcutta, the mirror neurons firing in our brains let us know what it may feel like to be a part of that embrace, the oxytocin released in our bodies makes us feel connected with everyone around us, and the warm feeling of elevation that Jonathan Haidt talks about wells up in our chest and motivates us to act with similar kindness and compassion.

Thus, there are at least three different ways that we can focus our Appreciation of Beauty and Excellence – on physical beauty, on human excellence in others and ourselves, and on acts of love, kindness, and compassion that can awaken and bring the better angels within us, that Lincoln talked about, to life.

This is the power of appreciation. You drive a new car off the lot and it quickly depreciates by thousands of dollars that you will never get back. Then you see or just think about something beautiful or the love that someone expressed to you and that depreciating car, downturn in the stock market, or even that cancer diagnosis you recently got no longer bother you quite so much.

Moreover, gratitude may just be a different facet of appreciation where both stem from the same wondrous capacity we have to see, savor, and be moved by the things around us. The word gratitude is derived from the same root word as "grace" – as in that which can be amazing – and which refers to something that is a free gift.

Gratitude is a natural response to receiving a gift and it motivates us to give back in some way. There are times when there is a person that we can thank for a gift we receive, like you do when you write a gratitude letter. But there are other times when we can't attribute what we are grateful for to another human being. Maybe that's why some of us can't help but think that there might be something sacred or divine behind it all.

But even if we can't always identify the source of what we are grateful for, we can use our motivation to give back to increase the courage and grit we need for doing some of the hard things we sometimes have to do. Gratitude can enable us to extend our empathy and compassion to those who are more difficult to love – or help us face our fears and overcome the obstacles that get in the way of our goals and dreams.

While I gave you ways to increase your Appreciation of Beauty and Excellence by knowing where to look, I want to leave you with some of the specific ways we have found that may help us the most in fostering gratitude.

First, research has shown that there are benefits in simply stopping to count our blessings and that, for most people, it doesn't have to be every day. We may want to start by creating a working list of all the different things we are grateful for; but returning once a week to review, remind ourselves, and add to the list may go a long way.

Second, the thing we that asked you to do during the first part of this challenge - to look for three good things every day - may be good to do more often. We can use it whenever we sense that negativity bias beginning to creep back into our awareness and make it harder for us to see and appreciate the little things that can bring us so much joy.

Third, there is the expression of gratitude that was a part of the gratitude letter you wrote and all of the other ways that we can intentionally say the words that can mean so much to other people. You can continue this in so many ways and use the new vocabulary of the VIA strengths you have learned and strength spotting to better see what you can express to others in gratitude.

There are countless other small and simple ways we can remind ourselves of the goodness, beauty, kindness, and love that can help get us out of bed on our darkest days. You can start a gratitude journal that you review when you feel the storm clouds rolling in. You can write the blessings you have counted or good things you have noticed on *Post-Its* or enter them as reminders on one of the many smart phone apps that now make this possible. You can make it a part of your routine to send an email or give a note of appreciation to someone at the beginning or end of every week or every day.

Gratitude is like the kindness that we talked about in relation to the movie Amélie. It is one of the most powerful ways to change our lives and raise our happiness to a new level – and once we begin to see its power and experience its benefits – we won't want to stop practicing it.

Workbook Tasks for the Chapter

Here are the tasks that will continue to help you plan for a better future, deal with the stress and obstacles along the way, and foster appreciation and gratitude:

First, as after every chapter, there is a link to a video where you can see and hear me going over the lesson for this chapter.

Second, there is a special video to watch from the movie *The Shawshank Redemption* that shows how it is possible to appreciate beauty in almost any circumstance and that doing so can make all the difference.

Third, the most important task for this chapter is to complete the final two steps of the PATH process using the guidelines in Appendix K. This includes step 7, Organizing the Month's Work, by being specific about how you'll make progress in the next month, and step 8, Committing to the First Step, which involves identifying and doing something now to get started.

Fourth, the next task involves giving yourself a kind of psychological vaccination with something called *Stress Inoculation Training* developed by psychologist Donald Meichenbaum. Here, it will involve making a list of the obstacles that you may face in pursuing your PATH goals and writing about how you might best deal with them.

Fifth, there are reflection questions about how to make appreciation and gratitude more a part of your life and about taking the first step you set for yourself in the PATH process.

1. Author Video for this Lesson

Here is the link for the video of me going over the lesson for this chapter.

https://youtu.be/Ce0RdjOEbjI

2. Special Video – "The Shawshank Redemption Opera Scene"

Watch the video and think about how you could use the Appreciation Beauty and Excellence to help get through some of the stressful events you may face in the future.

https://www.youtube.com/watch?v=qzuM2XTnpSA

3. Finishing the PATH Process

Complete the 7th and 8th steps and final step of the PATH process as described in the Guidelines for the PATH Process in Appendix K. The 7th step is called Organizing the Month's Work and involves being specific about what you will do to make progress in walking your path in the next month. The 8th step is called Committing to the First Step and involves one thing you can do to get started with the PATH you have envisioned for yourself. In order to fully understand these steps and what to aim for, be sure to watch the videos that Appendix K provides the links for if you haven't already.

4. Stress Inoculation Training for Potential Obstacles

This task involves practicing a kind of psychological vaccination developed by psychologist Donald Meichenbaum called *Stress Inoculation Training.*

First, make a list of 3-5 obstacles or kinds of stress that you think may get in the way of your being successful in achieving your goals and realizing the best possible life that you are aiming for in the PATH process.

Second, write about how you might best do something to cope with each of the obstacles or stressors that you identify. If it helps, go back and review any lessons in the workbook that may particularly help you come with ideas such as the chapters on mindfulness, resilience, perseverance, and self-efficacy.

___

___

___

___

5. Reflection Questions

What can you do to make appreciation or gratitude more a part of your life? How could you make them a part of your routine in way that might enable them to become a habit for you? You might want to review the suggestions near the end of this chapter for different ways to practice gratitude.

What is the first step you identified to take in beginning the PATH process? Where and when can you take it?

____

____

____

____

____

____

____

What happened when you took the first step in the PATH process? How did it affect you? What might be a good next step to take?

____

____

____

____

____

____

____

____

Chapter 23

Meaning and Purpose

He who has a "why" to live for can bear almost any "how."

— Friedrich Nietzsche

Welcome to our second to last chapter! I hope that working through the PATH process in creating your poster has been a valuable experience for you. This process can be a wonderful way to chart your course to a better future and apply what you have learned in this challenge. It may be good to know that you can shift and change and create another PATH poster as you gain more perspective on your life, as different things happen in your life, or as you meet new challenges or see new opportunities.

The main thing is that the PATH process can give you permission to dream, identify goals and ways to accomplish them, and use what you have learned to make it happen. One very important thing we want to make sure you take time to do is to follow through in inviting and enrolling people on your "dream team" to support, encourage, and help you make progress. Even though you may hesitate to ask, giving someone else the chance to help you make the most of your life can be a gift that brings great meaning to theirs.

All of which brings us to today's topic, Meaning and Purpose, which is the last lesson before our review and celebration in the final chapter of this challenge. Meaning and Purpose is the only thing that is both included as a strength in the VIA classification and as one of the elements of well-being in the PERMA theory of well-being. So, it can be both a strength that is a means to an end and also an end that we seek for its own sake. In fact, you might even think about meaning and purpose as the very essence of a life worth living.

I've talked about the role that Viktor Frankl played in bringing meaning and purpose to the forefront of positive psychology. There is an interesting fact about his well-known book titled *Man's Search for Meaning.* This is where he writes about how a sense of meaning and purpose enabled him to survive four concentration camps in Nazi Germany and about his approach to helping people increase meaning in their lives.

In the early years of positive psychology, there was a poll about what was the best positive psychology book. Even though *Man's Search for Meaning* was written a half a century before Martin Seligman because using the phrase "positive psychology," it was voted the best book - and for good reason. There are more than a few memorable things that Frankl has to say that demonstrate the insights and wisdom you can find in that book. One is how he expands on the famous quote by Friedrich Nietzsche that we began this chapter with, "those who have a 'why' to live, can bear almost any 'how'."

In *Man's Search for Meaning,* Frankl writes about one of the biggest things that gave him a "why" to bear the horrors he saw and experienced in those concentration camps. He wrote about how having to trudge through the mud on the many cold and rainy days to work led to exhaustion and death for many of his fellow prisoners. He wrote about what gave him the meaning to endure so many of the horrible days when those around him were losing their will to live.

He would imagine and hold in his mind one of the greatest gifts that he believed he had received and that made his life worth living - the love of his wife. Even though he didn't know if she was even still alive, it was the thought there could be a love like that which kept him alive. It preserved his will to live and gave him a reason to go on and write a book about the power of meaning and purpose so you and I could read about it today.

The other big thing that Frankl has to say lies that the heart of this challenge and brings us back to the poet Mary Oliver's big question: "What is it you plan to do with your one wild and precious life?" That is one famous question in the form of a quote and here is Frankl's famous answer in the same form. He said this in three simple lines:

"Between stimulus and response there is a space.
In that space is our power to choose our response.
In our response lies our growth and our freedom."

The purpose of this challenge is to help you see that space, the power of the choice you can make and, if you are willing to make it, help you develop a vision and plan for what to do with the opportunity for growth and freedom that you now have in your "one wild and precious life."

Before finishing this chapter, there are three things I want to say about how meaning and purpose can help us answer this question. First, the kind of meaning and purpose we are talking about here is not the same as the pleasure that so many associate with happiness. Pleasure and positive emotions can be wonderful gifts of life in our lives that are worth appreciating and being grateful for as we discussed in the last chapter.

But if pleasure was the only thing that was important to Frankl, he may not have survived to go on to write that book. If it were all that we sought, then there might be many things that bring meaning to our lives that we might never do - like having kids, going to college, being a caregiver, serving our country, taking a stand for what we believe in, or having many of the goals and dreams that you may have expressed when you wrote about your best possible life or completed your PATH poster.

Meaning is more than just pleasure and it enables us not only to survive but to thrive – and can be an essential part of what it means to thrive. It gives us something to live for even when pleasure can be hard to find – like during a pandemic, when we have chronic pain or a chronic illness, when our relationship ends, when we lose a loved one, or when we don't get that promotion. When pleasure is waning like it may at times during our periods of greatest stress; it is the meaning we get from those special people, experiences, places, and projects in our lives that make all the difference, get us through, and make it all worth it.

Second, although the kind of meaning and purpose we are talking about can be found in spirituality and organized religion, it is not necessarily the same thing and can also be found in other ways. The word religion has come to be associated with those of us that organize their lives around a traditional set of beliefs and practices. The word spirituality has come to take on a different, broader meaning sometimes associated with God or a higher power – but increasingly more often with nature, the universe, or a higher cause or purpose.

The kind of meaning and purpose we are talking about here may or may not involve organized religion and related forms of spirituality, but it always involves what makes us want to be alive, get up in the morning, and follow the advice that Robin William gives his class in the movie *Dead Poet Society:* "carpe diem," which is Latin for "seize the day!"

Third, like the love Victor Frankl experienced with his wife, to have that sense of meaning and purpose – or even to be on the quest to find it, can enable us to focus our lives in a world where we are pulled in so many directions, and put us on a path to making the most of our lives. There are several ways that we have tried to enable you to do this in this challenge. We have tried to encourage you to find what you love to do, what your strengths are, who and what you are grateful for, what kinds of causes you may want to be involved with and give back to, and what you most want your life to be like in the future.

Viktor Frankl has given us the gift of seeing our lives not only as the pursuit of pleasure, but with the larger perspective of the meaning and purpose that can inspire and motivate us through the hardest of times, not only to survive but also to thrive and flourish - and to truly make our lives worth living.

Workbook Tasks for the Chapter

The tasks are designed to enable you to better understand and foster meaning and purpose in your life and think about how you can share the benefits of what you have learned in this challenge with others:

First, as after every chapter, there is a link to a video where you can see and hear me going over the lesson for this chapter.

Second, there is a special video about the core message of Viktor Frankl's book *Man's Search for Meaning* about the value of a sense of meaning and purpose in our lives. This was included to help you reflect on the meaning in your life and how meaning might be a part of the future that you may want to work towards.

Third, there is a task that involves writing about the most meaningful things that you have learned or done as part of this challenge and how they might change your life for the better.

Fourth, there are reflection questions about how your life might be different if you focused more time and energy on what brings meaning and purpose to your life. Identifying and focusing on the benefits of a more meaningful life will help motivate you to achieve it.

Fifth, there is a task about "paying it forward" that involves writing about how you can pass what you have learned about and done in the challenge on to others and how you might make expressing gratitude and kindness a bigger part of your life.

1. Author's Video for this Chapter

Here is the link for the video of me going over the lesson for this chapter.

https://youtu.be/egdvtk99GyE

2. Special Video – "Man's Search for Meaning by Viktor Frankl/Core Message"

Watch the video and think about what may bring you more meaning in the future and how meaning might be more a part of the best possible life and future you may have envisioned in the PATH process.

https://www.youtube.com/watch?v=YYBg9_069gg

3. Reflection Questions

What you think are the most meaningful things that you learned as a part of this challenge?

____

____

____

____

____

____

____

____

____

____

How do you think you might use them to change your life for the better?

4. The Benefits of a Meaningful Life

How might your life be different if you focused more time and energy on what can bring meaning and purpose to your life? What would you be focusing on and doing?

5. Paying It Forward

What you could do to pay what you have learned and done in this workbook forward and pass it on to other people and causes you care about?

Who would you most like to share something you learned or one of the activities you benefited from? What would you like share and how could you do it?

____

____

____

____

____

____

____

____

How could you make expressing gratitude and kindness to others an increasing and more regular and routine part of your life?

____

____

____

____

____

____

____

____

Chapter 24

Review and Celebration

Two roads diverged in a wood and I –
I took the one less traveled by,
and that has made all the difference.
— Robert Frost

Welcome to our final chapter! You are almost there. I hope you feel good for having made it this far. Of course, the challenge to make the most of your life never really ends. Just as when you began this challenge you were answering a call to adventure into unknown territory, so you will experience this call in new ways as you continue your journey after you have completed this workbook.

What I would like to do in this last chapter is to help you reflect on what you have learned so you can savor it and begin to imagine how you can carry it with you as you continue on the path you may have mapped out for yourself in the PATH process.

The first big thing we wanted to do in the challenge was to give you a way to think about and identify what may really make you happy and enable you to make the most of your life. We started by introducing positive psychology as the science of happiness and what makes life worth living. We gave you an idea of all we are learning about what makes most people happy so you would have a good background for thinking about and identifying what may make you most happy so you can begin to make it more a part of your life.

We talked about how Martin Seligman, who as the president of the American Psychological Association, started the initiative that became positive psychology back in 1998. Positive psychology was founded to increase the focus on what makes us happy, enables us to become our best, and live our lives to the fullest.

We learned about how psychology had fallen into our very human negativity bias where we pay so much attention to the potential threats in our lives – that we may miss many of the good things that can help us deal with these threats. Seligman developed that PERMA theory we keep going back to that says there may be at least five different elements that make up human happiness and well-being:

1. Positive emotions – such as joy, interest, love, and contentment.
2. Engagement - which includes the experience of flow.
3. Relationships - where we experience so much of our happiness.
4. Meaning - which may be the essence of a life worth living.
5. Accomplishment - which is our desire to master and do things well for its own sake.

One of the tasks you will have for this chapter is to take the same well-being survey we suggested for the first chapter of the challenge so you can compare your scores on the elements of PERMA and see how they may have changed. But remember that PERMA is a general theory that may miss some of the specific things that may make you as a unique person most happy. So, if there is something else you envisioned for your path or best possible life, please feel free to make it a focus for you and think about how it may have changed during your time working through this challenge.

Thus, the first big thing we tried to do was to enable you think about and see more clearly what would might make you happy, what you want the most, and what might be your best possible life. The second thing that we spent most of our time on was offering you the tools that modern science, psychology, and positive psychology have discovered and made available so we can better accomplish our goals and realize our best possible life.

As part of your basic training during the first part of this challenge, you learned about the power of positive reappraisal, behavioral activation, and facing your fears, how to practice mindfulness to be more present to your life, how to increase resilience and stress-related growth, and how to foster your inherent capacity for wisdom and creativity.

As part of helping you better see, embrace, and use the best in yourself to make the most of your life, during the second part of the challenge we gave you new ways to identify and use your strengths. We also focused on how you can build and use the strengths that may be most important in enabling you to move forward in your journey – including authenticity, perseverance, courage, self-efficacy, and self-control.

As part of your living and being a part of a social network and larger community, during the third part we focused on how you can improve your relationships with others and find better ways to have a positive impact on the community and world around you. Specifically, we examined social intelligence and how you can build and use love, kindness, fairness, justice, and forgiveness to a create community that gives us the chance to thrive together.

In this fourth and final part of the challenge, you have had the opportunity to put it all together in writing about your best possible life and using the PATH process to plan and map out your way forward after this challenge. In this part, we focused on strengths like optimism and hope, humor, appreciation and gratitude, and meaning and purpose - which make it possible for us to rise above some of the limitations of the lives we have known and begin to see and realize more of the kind of life we want most

We hope that you have had the opportunity to watch some of the videos that we created especially for this challenge and that you will feel free to return to them as often as you like to refresh yourself in what you have been learning (a complete listing of the Author Videos is in Appendix C). We also hope that you will remember and revisit the other videos that really spoke to you. Maybe it was the symphony coming together to play the Ode to Joy in a public square, Heather Dorniden getting up to win that race, Maya Angelou talking about how love liberates, the little six year old girl giving wise advice to her mother, the boy with autism making those six 3 pointers in a row, appreciating the beauty of the singing in *The Shawshank Redemption*, or Lily when she found out that she was going to Disneyland (a complete listing of these other Special Videos can be found in Appendix D.)

Most of all, we hope that you will find ways to continue to incorporate and benefit from the exercises that helped you the most. Whether it is finding ways to continue to see, create, and savor the good things around you; use your strengths in new ways and experience the wind at our back; ways to share kindness and gratitude with those around you; or finding more meaning in becoming a part of a cause or something greater than yourself that expands the reach of love, kindness, and compassion to others. Whatever it may have been, we hope that you will find ways to further pursue and continue to build on the lessons, activities, and videos that spoke to you and made the most difference for you.

Finally, I hope you will take the time to congratulate yourself, savor, and celebrate the good work you have done; give yourself any time you may need to rest, recover, and rejuvenate; and to then to follow through in moving forward on your path toward making the most of your one wild and precious life!

Workbook Tasks for the Chapter

These are the tasks that can help you to review and celebrate what you have learned in this challenge and how it may have affected your happiness and well-being.

First, as after every chapter, there is a link to a video where you can see and hear me going over the lesson for this chapter.

Second, there is a special video about gratitude by Louie Schwartzberg, who is a well-known cinematographer who has focused on capturing beauty. This video is about how we can use gratitude to make every day a good day.

Third, there are reflection questions about how you can remember what you have learned in this challenge and follow through in pursuing your best possible life.

Fourth, there is a task that involves identifying what you can do to celebrate and reward yourself for having completed this challenge - and then doing it!

Finally, there is an opportunity to take the well-being survey that you took in the first chapter of this challenge. Completing and scoring this will enable you to compare your scores to see what may have changed for you. You can also feel free to make copies of the survey so that you can use it whenever you want in monitoring your progress in the future.

Our Gratitude and Best Wishes!

Most important, on behalf everyone who contributed to making this challenge and workbook possible, I wanted to thank you for taking part and being open to the lessons and activities that have meant so much to us and so many of our students and colleagues. It has been a great pleasure and joy to be with you in this positive psychology challenge.

We wish you the best in finding whatever happiness you seek, in realizing a life that for you is truly worth living, and in continuing on your path of making the most of your life and living it the fullest!

1. Author's Video for this Lesson

Here is the link for the video of me going over the lesson for this chapter.

https://youtu.be/eOC_GZ5KcGo

2. Special Video - "Gratitude | Louie Schwartzberg"

Watch the video and think about how you can better exercise gratitude to make every one of your days a good day.

https://www.youtube.com/watch?v=gXDMoiEkyuQ

3. Reflection Questions

How can you remember and remind yourself about the most important and meaningful things you have learned about and done as a part of this challenge? Some examples of ways may be to return to, review, or redo parts of the workbook at regular intervals, create computer or smart phone reminders of the most important lessons for you, or make a schedule for continuing to practice the activities that were most beneficial to you.

____

____

____

____

____

____

____

____

____

____

____

What can you do to help you follow through in achieving your best possible life and the goals that you set for yourself in the PATH process? Some examples of what you could do might include creating a schedule for working towards specific goals, meeting regularly with members of your PATH "dream team" to report progress and get their support, and identifying ways to celebrate and reward yourself for the progress that you make.

4. Celebrate Completing the Challenge!

Write about what you can do to celebrate and reward yourself for having completed this challenge. Then take the time to do it!

5. Complete the Well-Being Survey

Complete and score the survey below. This is the same survey that you may have completed at the end of the first chapter. If you completed that initial survey, then you can now compare your scores at the beginning and end of the challenge. (There is an additional copy of this survey that you can complete as many times as you want in Appendix E).

Instructions: First, circle the number that best indicates your response for each question. Second, add up your scores for the five elements of well-being (positive emotions, engagement, relationships, meaning, and accomplishment) and for negative emotions. Third, see what the scores mean in the table below and compare these to your earlier scores.

1. In general, to what extent do you lead a purposeful and meaningful life?

   Not at all 0 1 2 3 4 5 6 7 8 9 10 Completely

2. How much of the time do you feel you are making progress towards accomplishing your goals?

   Never 0 1 2 3 4 5 6 7 8 9 10 Always

3. How often do you become absorbed in what you are doing?

   Never 0 1 2 3 4 5 6 7 8 9 10 Always

4. In general, how often do you feel joyful?

   Never 0 1 2 3 4 5 6 7 8 9 10 Always

5. To what extent do you receive help and support from others when you need it?

   Not at all 0 1 2 3 4 5 6 7 8 9 10 Completely

6. In general, how often do you feel anxious?

   Never 0 1 2 3 4 5 6 7 8 9 10 Always

7. How often do you achieve the important goals you have set for yourself?

   Never 0 1 2 3 4 5 6 7 8 9 10 Always

8. In general, to what extent do you feel that what you do in your life is valuable and worthwhile?

   Not at all 0 1 2 3 4 5 6 7 8 9 10 Completely

9. In general, how often do you feel positive?

   Never 0 1 2 3 4 5 6 7 8 9 10 Always

10. In general, to what extent do you feel excited and interested in things?

    Not at all 0 1 2 3 4 5 6 7 8 9 10 Completely

11. In general, how often do you feel angry?

Never 0 1 2 3 4 5 6 7 8 9 10 Always

12. To what extent have you been feeling loved?

Not at all 0 1 2 3 4 5 6 7 8 9 10 Completely

13. How often are you able to handle your responsibilities?

Never 0 1 2 3 4 5 6 7 8 9 10 Always

14. To what extent do you generally feel you have a sense of direction in your life?

Not at all 0 1 2 3 4 5 6 7 8 9 10 Completely

15. How satisfied are you with your personal relationships?

Not at all 0 1 2 3 4 5 6 7 8 9 10 Completely

16. In general, how often do you feel sad?

Never 0 1 2 3 4 5 6 7 8 9 10 Always

17. How often do you lose track of time while doing something you enjoy?

Never 0 1 2 3 4 5 6 7 8 9 10 Always

18. In general, to what extent do you feel contented?

Not at all 0 1 2 3 4 5 6 7 8 9 10 Completely

Add up the total for each of the three questions for following:

_____ Positive Emotions (4, 9, 18)
_____ Engagement (3, 10, 17)
_____ Relationships (5, 12, 15)
_____ Meaning (1, 8, 14)
_____ Accomplishment (2, 7, 13)
_____ Negative Emotions (6, 11, 16)

Level of Well-Being	Ranges for Positive Emotions, Engagement, Relationships, Meaning & Accomplishment	Ranges for Negative Emotions
Very high	27-30	0-3
High	24-26	4-9
Average	20-23	10-15
Low	15-19	16-19
Very low	0-14	20-30

If you like, you can take the survey online and read more about it at the following address: https://www.authentichappiness.sas.upenn.edu/questionnaires/perma

Appendix A: Additional Readings

Biswas-Diener, R. (2010). *Practicing positive psychology coaching: Assessment, activities, and strategies for success.* Hoboken, NJ: John Wiley & Sons.

Brown, B. (2012). *Daring greatly: How the courage to be vulnerable transforms the way we live, love, parent, and lead.* New York: Gotham Books.

Burns, D. (2008). *Feeling good: The new mood therapy.* New York: Harper.

Campbell, J. (1949). *The hero with a thousand faces.* Princeton, N.J.: Princeton University Press.

Campbell, J. (2004). *Pathways to bliss: Mythology and personal transformation.* Novato, CA: New World Press.

Csikszentmihalyi, M. (1990). *Flow: The psychology of optimal experience.* New York: Harper Perennial.

Emmons, R.A. (2013). *Gratitude works: A 21-day program for creating emotional prosperity.* San Francisco, CA: Jossey-Bass.

Enright, R.D. (2001). *Forgiveness is a choice: A step-by-step process for resolving anger and restoring hope.* Washington, DC: American Psychological Association.

Frankl, V. E. (1963). *Man's search for meaning.* New York: Pocket Books.

Froh, J.J., & Parks, A.C. (2013). *Activities for teaching positive psychology: A guide for instructors.* Washington, DC: American Psychological Association.

Haidt, J. (2006). *The happiness hypothesis: Finding modern truth in ancient wisdom.* New York: Basic Books.

Hanson, R. (2013). *Hardwiring happiness: The new brain science of contentment, calm, and confidence.* New York: Harmony Books.

Joseph, S. (Ed.). (2015). *Positive psychology in practice: Promoting human flourishing in work, health, education, and everyday life.* Hoboken, NJ: John Wiley & Sons.

Kabat-Zinn, J. (1994). *Wherever you go, there you are.* New York: Hyperion.

Keltner, D. (2010). The compassionate instinct. In D. Keltner, J. Marsh & J.A. Smith. *The compassionate instinct* (pp. 8-15). New York: W.W. Norton.

Lopez, S.J., & Snyder, C.R. (Eds.). (2009). *Oxford handbook of positive psychology* (2nd Ed.). New York: Oxford University Press.

Lyubomirsky, S. (2007). *The how of happiness: A new approach to getting the life you want.* New York: Penguin Books.

Miller, W.R., & C'de Baca, J. (2001). *Quantum change: When epiphanies and sudden insights transform ordinary lives.* New York: Guilford Press.

Mumford, G. (2015). *The mindful athlete: Secrets to pure performance.* Berkeley, CA: Parallax Press.

Neff, K. (2011). *Self-compassion: The proven power of being kind to yourself.* New York: HarperCollins.

Niemiec, R.M. (2014). *Mindfulness and character strengths: A practical guide to flourishing.* Boston, MA: Hogrefe Publishing.

Niemiec, R.M. (2014). *Positive psychology at the movies: Using films to build character strengths and well-being* (2nd Ed.). Boston, MA: Hogrefe Publishing.

Niemiec, R.M. (2018). *Character strengths interventions: A field guide for practitioners.* Boston, MA: Hogrefe.

O'Hanlon, B., & Bertolino, B. (2012). *The therapist's notebook on positive psychology: Activities, exercises, and handouts.* New York: Routledge.

Pearpoint, J., O'Brien, J., & Forest, M. (2011). *PATH: A workbook for planning positive possible futures.* Toronto, CA: Inclusion Press.

Pennebaker, J.W., & Smyth, J.M. (2016). *Opening up by writing it down: How expressive writing improves health and eases emotional pain* (3rd Ed.). New York: Guilford Press.

Peterson, C., & Seligman, M.E.P. (2004). *Character strengths and virtues: A handbook of classification.* New York: Oxford University Press.

Polly, S. & Britton, K. (Eds.). (2015). *Character strengths matter: How to live a full life.* Positive

Post, S., & Neimark, J. (2007). *Why good things happen to good people.* New York: Broadway Books.

Proctor, C., & Eades, J.F. (2016). *Strengths gym: Build and exercise your strengths.* Channel Islands, GYI 6HL: Positive Psychology Research Centre.

Rashid, T., & Seligman, M. (2018). *Positive psychotherapy: Clinical manual.* New York: Oxford University Press.

Rashid, T., & Seligman, M. (2019). *Positive psychotherapy: Workbook.* New York: Oxford

Rogers, C.R. (1995). *On becoming a person* (2nd Ed.). New York: Mariner Books.

Seligman, M.E.P. (2002). *Authentic happiness: Using the new positive psychology to realize your potential for lasting fulfillment.* New York: Free Press.

Seligman, M.E.P. (2011). *Flourish: A visionary new understanding of happiness and well-being.* New York: Free Press.

Smith, B.W. (2018). *Positive psychology for the hero's journey: Discovering true and lasting happiness.* Seattle, WA: Kindle Direct Publishing.

Smith, B.W. (2020). The hero's journey to resilience and thriving in the context of disaster. In Stefan Schulenberg (Ed.), *Positive Psychology and Disaster Mental Health (pp. 81-98).* New York: Springer.

Smith, B.W., Ford, C.G., Erickson, K., & Guzman, A. (2020). The effects of a character strength focused positive psychology course on undergraduate happiness and well-being. *Journal of Happiness Studies.* https://doi.org/10.1007/s10902-020-00233-9

Snyder, C.R. (1994). *The psychology of hope: You can get there from here.* New York: Free Press.

Snyder, C.R., Lopez, S.J., & Pedrotti, J. T. (2015). *Positive psychology: The Scientific and practical explorations of human strengths, 3rd edition.* Sage: Thousand Oaks, CA.

Worthington, E.L. (2001). *Five steps to forgiveness: The art and science of forgiving.* New York: Crown Publishing.

Appendix B: Positive Psychology Activities

Here is a list of the main positive psychology activities for each chapter of the challenge. The focus is on seeing and creating more good things in Part 1, identifying and using your top strengths in Part 2, expressing gratitude, kindness, and contributing to a cause in Part 3, and creating a vision and road map to your best possible life in Part 4.

Part 1: Basic Training for Your Best Life

Chapter	Primary Exercise	Secondary Exercise
1	Identify good things during the day	Complete and score a well-being survey
2	Identify and remind yourself of good things	Answer questions about what makes you happy
3	Identify and look forward to good things	Identify and do your new pleasant things to try from a list
4	Identify and appreciate good things	Do a guided mindful breathing meditation
5	Identify and plan to create more good things	Write about when you were and would like to be resilient
6	Identify and plan to continue to find and create good things	Complete the wheel of life exercise to see how balanced your life is

Part 2: Bringing Out the Best in Yourself

Chapter	Primary Exercise	Secondary Exercise
7	Take the VIA Survey to identify your strengths and give examples	Practice spotting strengths in other people
8	Use two of your top strengths in a new way	Plan new ways to use each of your top strengths
9	Use one of your top strengths to experience flow in a new way	Identify how you can use your top strengths to be happy
10	Use a top strength in a new way to benefit someone else	Write about a time when you showed courage
11	Use a top strength in a new way to reach a goal	Develop a plan for increasing self-efficacy where you need it
12	Identify things you'd like to savor and try at least one	Develop a plan for increasing self-control where you need it

Part 3: Bringing Out the Best around You

Chapter	Primary Exercise	Secondary Exercise
13	Reflect about a relationship and do something to improve it	Make of list of who you are grateful to and why
14	Write and share a gratitude letter	Take the Languages of Love survey and think about how it can help you
15	Do a new kind act for someone you know	Identify and plan acts of kinds for friends and strangers
16	Do a new kind act for a stranger	Identify groups appreciate and a cause you'd like to contribute to
17	Do something to support a cause that is important to you	Identify ways to express love and kindness to yourself and try one
18	Write about a time you were hurt and the benefits of forgiveness	Develop a plan for forgiving yourself when you make a mistake

Part 4: Creating the Best Possible Future

Chapter	Primary Exercise	Secondary Exercise
19	Begin the PATH process and do steps 1 and 2	Write about your best possible life in the future
20	Do steps 3 and 4 of the PATH process	Identify things you have learned to help achieve your best possible life
21	Do steps 5 and 6 of the PATH process	Create a plan to use what you learned for your best possible life
22	Do steps 7 and 8 of the PATH process	Prepare for coping with future stress and obstacles
23	Develop a plan to "pay forward" what you have learned	Write about the benefits of a more meaningful life
24	Develop a plan for continuing to benefit from what you learned	Complete the well-being survey a second time and compare your scores

Appendix C: Links to Author Videos

Chapter 1: A Call to Adventure - https://youtu.be/rwYpX8ua8vs

Chapter 2: What Do You Want Most? - https://youtu.be/ccM094t4Cas

Chapter 3: How Can You Make It Happen? - https://youtu.be/8ZDDcz5D5Vo

Chapter 4: Mindfulness and Acceptance - https://youtu.be/S_dAoCZe-W4

Chapter 5: Resilience and Stress-Related Growth - https://youtu.be/2dndl9JI51E

Chapter 6: Wisdom and Creativity - https://youtu.be/BYyAVCBnEqE

Chapter 7: Discovering Your Best - https://youtu.be/PCxzb3G_eiE

Chapter 8: Authenticity - https://youtu.be/iTvmXXRKJLY

Chapter 9: Perseverance - https://youtu.be/v_UuF1g1jP8

Chapter 10: Courage - https://youtu.be/2gOSNDKB3CM

Chapter 11: Self-Efficacy - https://youtu.be/zHlEEC_kwgU

Chapter 12: Self-Control - https://youtu.be/t2TtNgrGYbY

Chapter 13: Social Intelligence - https://youtu.be/PxI6jFYcGA4

Chapter 14: Love - https://youtu.be/D7igjMBjqSk

Chapter 15: Kindness - https://youtu.be/P7lnMXdEbNQ

Chapter 16: Community Positive Psychology - https://youtu.be/7nDAjP5Jf2g

Chapter 17: Fairness and Justice - https://youtu.be/YO4QaE4Dxmk

Chapter 18: Forgiveness - https://youtu.be/Ex5mrm2P8Pg

Chapter 19: The PATH Process - https://youtu.be/4DQaekZLyZs

Chapter 20: Optimism and Hope - https://youtu.be/Dd1bvK5xPck

Chapter 21: Humor - https://youtu.be/XMB19WU8Wr4

Chapter 22: Appreciation and Gratitude - https://youtu.be/Ce0RdjOEbjI

Chapter 23: Meaning and Purpose - https://youtu.be/egdvtk99GyE

Chapter 24: Review and Celebration - https://youtu.be/eOC_GZ5KcGo

Appendix D: Links to Special Videos

Chapter 1: A Call to Adventure
"What makes a hero? - Matthew Winkler"
https://www.youtube.com/watch?v=Hhk4N9A0oCA&t=21s

Chapter 2: What Do You Want Most?
"Alan Watts – What Do You Desire?"
https://www.youtube.com/watch?v=JCUFs2qJ1bs

Chapter 3: How Can You Make It Happen?
"Shawn Achor - The Happiness Advantage"
https://www.youtube.com/watch?v=GXy__kBVq1M

Chapter 4: Mindfulness and Acceptance
"Flashmob – Ode an die Freude (Ode to Joy)"
https://www.youtube.com/watch?v=kbJcQYVtZMo

Chapter 5: Resilience and Stress-Related Growth
"Heather Dorniden's Inspiring 600 meter race"
https://www.youtube.com/watch?v=70UF82nysIU

Chapter 6: Wisdom and Creativity
"The best gift I ever survived | Stacey Kramer"
https://www.youtube.com/watch?v=LgTnmWZX39w

Chapter 7: Discovering Your Best
"Good Will Hunting – Park scene subtitled"
https://www.youtube.com/watch?v=8GY-iWnriGg

Chapter 8: Authenticity
"The Power of Vulnerability | Brené Brown"
https://www.youtube.com/watch?v=iCvmsMzlF7o

Chapter 9: Perseverance
"Grit: the power of passion and perseverance | Angela Lee Duckworth"
https://www.youtube.com/watch?v=H14bBuluwB8

Chapter 10: Courage
"Adorable Girl Tells her Divorced Parents to be Friends"
https://www.youtube.com/watch?v=DCNUlEfD_dg

Chapter 11: Self-Efficacy
"The Most Inspirational Video You Will Ever See - Nick Vujicic's Story"
https://www.youtube.com/watch?v=Q6HnFuzSJdQ

Chapter 12: Self-Control
"Marshmallow Test – (funny)"
https://www.youtube.com/watch?v=Sc4EF3ijVJ8

Chapter 13: Social Intelligence
"Active Constructive Responding"
https://www.youtube.com/watch?v=qRORihbXMnA

Chapter 14: Love
"Dr. Maya Angelou - Love Liberates"
https://www.youtube.com/watch?v=cbecKv2xR14&t=89s

Chapter 15: Kindness
"The power of kindness: Johann Berlin"
https://www.youtube.com/watch?v=CG-SmD5X5Kk

Chapter 16: Community Positive Psychology
"RSA Animate: The Empathetic Civilisation" by Jeremy Rifkin
https://www.youtube.com/watch?v=l7AWnfFRc7g

Chapter 17: Fairness and Justice
"Two Monkeys Were Paid Unequally" by Frans de Waal
https://www.youtube.com/watch?v=meiU6TxysCg

Chapter 18: Forgiveness
"The power of forgiveness"
https://www.youtube.com/watch?v=o2BITY-3Mp4

Chapter 19: The PATH Process
"Lily's Disneyland Surprise!"
https://www.youtube.com/watch?v=OOpOhlGiRTM&t=67s

Chapter 20: Optimism and Hope
"Wow: Autistic Waterboy scores Non-Stop 3-pointers!"
https://www.youtube.com/watch?v=WV1akgvFknk

Chapter 21: Humor
"Human Behaviour experiment Lift Antics"
https://www.youtube.com/watch?v=XZDLbbfT9_Q

Chapter 22: Appreciation and Gratitude
"The Shawshank Redemption Opera Scene"
https://www.youtube.com/watch?v=qzuM2XTnpSA

Chapter 23: Meaning and Purpose
"Man's Search for Meaning by Viktor Frankl | Core Message"
https://www.youtube.com/watch?v=YYBg9_069gg

Chapter 24: Review and Celebration
"Gratitude | Louie Schwartzberg"
https://www.youtube.com/watch?v=gXDMoiEkyuQ

Appendix E: Well-Being Survey

This survey is used in Chapters 1 and 24 and you can use it as much as you want to monitor your progress in this challenge and to track changes in your happiness and well-being. If you like, you can take the survey online and read more about it at the following address:

https://www.authentichappiness.sas.upenn.edu/questionnaires/perma

Instructions: First, circle the number that best indicates your response for each question. Second, add up your scores for the five elements of well-being (positive emotions, engagement, relationships, meaning, and accomplishment) and for negative emotions. Third, see what the scores mean in the table below.

1. In general, to what extent do you lead a purposeful and meaningful life?

   Not at all 0 1 2 3 4 5 6 7 8 9 10 Completely

2. How much of the time do you feel you are making progress towards accomplishing your goals?

   Never 0 1 2 3 4 5 6 7 8 9 10 Always

3. How often do you become absorbed in what you are doing?

   Never 0 1 2 3 4 5 6 7 8 9 10 Always

4. In general, how often do you feel joyful?

   Never 0 1 2 3 4 5 6 7 8 9 10 Always

5. To what extent do you receive help and support from others when you need it?

   Not at all 0 1 2 3 4 5 6 7 8 9 10 Completely

6. In general, how often do you feel anxious?

   Never 0 1 2 3 4 5 6 7 8 9 10 Always

7. How often do you achieve the important goals you have set for yourself?

   Never 0 1 2 3 4 5 6 7 8 9 10 Always

8. In general, to what extent do you feel that what you do in your life is valuable and worthwhile?

   Not at all 0 1 2 3 4 5 6 7 8 9 10 Completely

9. In general, how often do you feel positive?

   Never 0 1 2 3 4 5 6 7 8 9 10 Always

10. In general, to what extent do you feel excited and interested in things?

    Not at all 0 1 2 3 4 5 6 7 8 9 10 Completely

11. In general, how often do you feel angry?

Never 0 1 2 3 4 5 6 7 8 9 10 Always

12. To what extent have you been feeling loved?

Not at all 0 1 2 3 4 5 6 7 8 9 10 Completely

13. How often are you able to handle your responsibilities?

Never 0 1 2 3 4 5 6 7 8 9 10 Always

14. To what extent do you generally feel you have a sense of direction in your life?

Not at all 0 1 2 3 4 5 6 7 8 9 10 Completely

15. How satisfied are you with your personal relationships?

Not at all 0 1 2 3 4 5 6 7 8 9 10 Completely

16. In general, how often do you feel sad?

Never 0 1 2 3 4 5 6 7 8 9 10 Always

17. How often do you lose track of time while doing something you enjoy?

Never 0 1 2 3 4 5 6 7 8 9 10 Always

18. In general, to what extent do you feel contented?

Not at all 0 1 2 3 4 5 6 7 8 9 10 Completely

Add up the total for each of the three questions for following:

_____ Positive Emotions (4, 9, 18)
_____ Engagement (3, 10, 17)
_____ Relationships (5, 12, 15)
_____ Meaning (1, 8, 14)
_____ Accomplishment (2, 7, 13)
_____ Negative Emotions (6, 11, 16)

Level of Well-Being	Ranges for Positive Emotions, Engagement, Relationships, Meaning & Accomplishment	Ranges for Negative Emotions
Very high	27-30	0-3
High	24-26	4-9
Average	20-23	10-15
Low	15-19	16-19
Very low	0-14	20-30

Appendix F: Pleasant Activities List

This list is used in Chapter 3.

1. Soaking in the bathtub
2. Planning my career
3. Getting out of (i.e., paying on) debt
4. Collecting things (coins, shells, etc.)
5. Going on vacation
6. Thinking how it will be when I finish school
7. Taking deep breaths
8. Recycling old items
9. Going on a date
10. Relaxing
11. Going to a movie in the middle of the week
12. Jogging, walking
13. Thinking I have done a full day's work
14. Listening to music
15. Buying household gadgets
16. Lying in the sun
17. Laughing
18. Thinking about my past trips
19. Listening to others
20. Reading magazines or newspapers
21. Hobbies (stamp collecting, model building)
22. Spending an evening with good friends
23. Planning a day's activities
24. Meeting new people
25. Remembering beautiful scenery
26. Saving money
27. Going home from work
28. Eating
29. Practicing karate, judo, yoga
30. Thinking about retirement
31. Repairing things around the house
32. Working on my car (bicycle)
33. Remembering the words and deeds of loving people
34. Wearing sexy clothes
35. Having quiet evenings
36. Taking care of my plants
37. Buying, selling stock
38. Going swimming
39. Doodling
40. Exercising
41. Collecting old things
42. Going to a party
43. Thinking about buying things
44. Playing golf
45. Playing soccer
46. Flying kites
47. Having discussions with friends
48. Having family get-togethers
49. Riding a motorcycle
50. Sex
51. Running
52. Going camping
53. Singing around the house
54. Arranging flowers
55. Practicing religion (going to church, group praying, etc.)
56. Losing weight
57. Going to the beach
58. Thinking I'm an OK person
59. A day with nothing to do
60. Going to reunions
61. Going skating
62. Going boating
63. Traveling abroad or in the U.S.

64. Painting
65. Doing something spontaneous
66. Doing needlepoint, knitting, cross-stitch, etc.
67. Sleeping
68. Driving
69. Entertaining
70. Going to clubs (garden, Parents without Partners, etc.)
71. Thinking about getting married
72. Going hunting
73. Singing with groups
74. Flirting
75. Playing musical instruments
76. Doing arts and crafts
77. Making a gift for someone
78. Buying records
79. Watching boxing, wrestling
80. Planning parties
81. Cooking
82. Going hiking
83. Writing short stories, novels, poems, or articles
84. Sewing
85. Buying clothes
86. Going out to dinner
87. Working
88. Discussing books
89. Sightseeing
90. Gardening
91. Going to the beauty parlor
92. Early morning coffee and newspaper
93. Playing tennis
94. Kissing
95. Watching children (play)
96. Thinking I have a lot more going for me than most people
97. Going to plays and concerts
98. Daydreaming
99. Planning to go to school
100. Thinking about sex
101. Driving or taking a train cross-country
102. Listening to the stereo
103. Refinishing furniture
104. Watching TV
105. Making lists of tasks
106. Going bike riding
107. Walks in the woods (or at the waterfront)
108. Giving gifts
109. Traveling to national parks
110. Completing a task
111. Watching a spectator sport (football, hockey, baseball)
112. Eating a favorite food
113. Teaching
114. Photography
115. Going fishing
116. Thinking about pleasant events
117. Playing with animals
118. Flying a plane
119. Reading fiction
120. Acting
121. Spending time by yourself
122. Writing diary entries or letters
123. Cleaning
124. Reading nonfiction
125. Taking children places
126. Dancing
127. Going on a picnic

128. Thinking "I did that pretty well" after doing something
129. Meditating
130. Playing volleyball
131. Having lunch with a friend
132. Going to the mountains
133. Thinking about people I like
134. Thoughts about happy moments in my childhood
135. Splurging
136. Playing cards
137. Solving riddles mentally
138. Having a political discussion
139. Playing softball
140. Seeing and/or showing photos or slides
141. Playing guitar
142. Doing crossword puzzles
143. Shooting pool
144. Dressing up and looking nice
145. Reflecting on how I've improved
146. Buying things for myself (perfume, golf balls, etc.)
147. Talking on the phone
148. Going to museums
149. Thinking religious thoughts
150. Lighting candles
151. Listening to the radio
152. Getting a massage
153. Saying "I love you"
154. Thinking about my good qualities
155. Buying books
156. Taking a sauna or a steam bath
157. Going skiing
158. White-water canoeing or rafting
159. Going bowling
160. Doing woodworking or carpentry
161. Fantasizing about the future
162. Taking ballet, tap dancing
163. Debating
164. Sitting in a sidewalk café
165. Having an aquarium
166. Going horseback riding
167. Thinking about becoming active in the community
168. Doing something new
169. Making jigsaw puzzles
170. Thinking I'm a person who can cope
171. Being in the country
172. Making contributions to religious, charitable, or other groups
173. Talking about sports
174. Meeting someone new
175. Listening to live music
176. Planning trips or vacations
177. Rock climbing or mountaineering
178. Reading the scriptures or other sacred works
179. Going to service, civic, or social club meetings
180. Rearranging or redecorating my room or house
181. Being naked
182. Reading a "How to Do It" article or book
183. Reading stories, novels, poems or plays
184. Going to lectures or hearing speakers
185. Writing a song or a piece of music
186. Saying something clearly
187. Doing something nice for my parents
188. Restoring antiques
189. Talking to myself
190. Working in politics
191. Working on machines
192. Completing a difficult task
193. Solving a problem, puzzle or crossword

194. Laughing
195. Going to a celebration
196. Shaving
197. Having lunch with friends or associates
198. Taking a shower
199. Riding in an airplane
200. Exploring the wilderness
201. Having a frank and open conversation
202. Thinking about myself or my life
203. Speaking or learning a foreign language
204. Going to a business meeting or a convention
205. Being in a sporty or expensive car
206. Cooking
207. Being helped
208. Wearing informal clothes
209. Combing or brushing my hair
210. Taking a nap
211. Canning, freezing, making preserves, etc.
212. Solving a personal problem
213. Being in a city
214. Singing to myself
215. Making food or crafts to sell or give away
216. Playing chess or checkers
217. Doing craftwork (pottery, jewelry, leather, beads and weaving)
218. Scratching myself
219. Putting on makeup
220. Designing or drafting
221. Visiting people who are sick, shut in, or in trouble
222. Cheering or rooting
223. Being popular at a gathering
224. Watching wild animals
225. Having an original idea
226. Landscaping or yardwork
227. Reading professional literature
228. Wearing new clothes
229. Just sitting and thinking
230. Seeing good things happen to my family and friends
231. Going to a fair, carnival, circus, zoo or amusement park
232. Talking about philosophy
233. Planning or organizing something
234. Listening to the sounds of nature
235. Dating or courting
236. Having a lively talk
237. Having friends come to visit
238. Playing sports
239. Introducing people who I think would like each other
240. Getting letters, cards or notes
241. Watching the clouds, sky or a storm
242. Going on outings to the park, a picnic, a barbecue, etc.
243. Giving a speech or a lecture
244. Reading maps
245. Gathering natural objects (rocks or driftwood)
246. Working on my finances
247. Wearing clean clothes
248. Making a major purchase or investment
249. Helping someone
250. Getting promoted
251. Hearing jokes
252. Talking about my children or grandchildren

253. Going to a crusade
254. Talking about good health
255. Seeing beautiful scenery
256. Eating good healthy meals
257. Improving my health (having my teeth fixed, getting new glasses, changing my diet)
258. Doing a job well
259. Having spare time
260. Loaning something
261. Being noticed as sexually attractive
262. Making others happy
263. Counseling someone
264. Going to a health club
265. Learning to do something new
266. Thinking about my parents
267. Supporting causes you believe in (social, political or environmental)
268. Kicking leaves, sand, pebbles, etc.
269. Playing lawn sports (badminton, croquet, bocce, horseshoes)
270. Seeing famous people
271. Going to the movies or renting one
272. Budgeting my time
273. Being praised by people I admire
274. Feeling a spiritual presence in my life
275. Doing a project in my own way
276. Doing odd jobs around the house
277. Crying
278. Being told I am needed
279. Being at a family reunion or get-together
280. Giving a party
281. Washing my hair
282. Coaching someone
283. Going to a restaurant
284. Seeing or smelling a flower or a plant
285. Being invited out
286. Receiving honors
287. Using perfume, cologne, or aftershave
288. Having someone agree with me
289. Reminiscing about old times
290. Getting up early in the morning
291. Having peace and quiet
292. Doing experiments and other scientific work
293. Visiting friends
294. Playing football
295. Being counseled
296. Saying prayers
297. Giving a massage
298. Taking adult education courses
299. Doing favors for people
300. Talking with people I enjoy
301. Being asked for help or advice
302. Helping other people solve their problems
303. Playing board games
304. Sleeping soundly at night
305. Snowmobile or dune buggy riding
306. Being in a support group
307. Dreaming at night
308. Playing ping-pong
309. Brushing my teeth
310. Walking barefoot
311. Playing Frisbee or catch
312. Doing housework or laundry
313. Petting and necking
314. Amusing people
315. Going to a barber or hair stylist
316. Having houseguests
317. Being with someone I love
318. Sleeping late
319. Starting a new project
320. Being assertive
321. Going to the library

322. Playing rugby or lacrosse
323. Birdwatching
324. Shopping
325. Playing video games or going to an arcade
326. People watching
327. Building or watching a fire
328. Selling or trading something
329. Finishing a project or task
330. Apologizing
331. Learning a new computer skill
332. Being a leader
333. Being with happy people
334. Playing games
335. Writing cards or notes
336. Asking for help or advice
337. Talking about my hobbies or special interests
338. Smiling at people
339. Playing in sand, a stream, the grass, etc.
340. Expressing my love to someone
341.Talking with friends over coffee or tea
342. Playing handball, paddleball, squash, etc.
343. "Surfing" the internet
344. Remembering a departed friend or loved one, visiting the cemetery
345. Staying up late
346. Going skiing or snowboarding
347. Having family members or friends do something that makes me proud of them
348. Going to auctions, garage sales, etc.
349. Thinking about an interesting question
350. Doing volunteer work, working on community service projects
351. Water skiing, surfing, and scuba diving
352. Defending or protecting someone; stopping fraud or abuse
353. Hearing a good sermon
354. Winning a competition
355. Making a new friend
356. Reading cartoons, comic strips or comic books
357. Borrowing something
358. Traveling in a group
359. Seeing old friends
360. Mentoring someone
361. Using my strength
362. Attending an opera or the ballet
363. Playing with pets
364. Looking at the stars or the moon
365. Being coached

Reference:

MacPhillamy, D. J., & Lewinsohn, P. M. (1982). The pleasant events schedule: Studies on reliability, validity, and scale intercorrelation. *Journal of Consulting and Clinical Psychology,* 50(3), 363-380.

Appendix G: Strength Spotting Tool

This tool is used in Chapter 7. Below are the 24 VIA character strengths. Which of these most strongly describes someone you know? Check off those strengths that you most clearly see in them. Choose about five strengths and no more than seven. Reflect on what they have done and/or said that makes you check one of the strengths for them. Let them know what you see if you can.

WISDOM

_____ **Creativity:** ingenuity; sees & does things in new/unique ways; original and adaptive ideas
_____ **Curiosity:** novelty-seeker; takes an interest; open to different experiences; asks questions
_____ **Open-mindedness & Judgment:** critical thinker; analytical; logical; thinks things through
_____ **Love of learning:** masters new skills & topics; passionate about knowledge & learning
_____ **Wisdom:** wise; provides wise counsel; sees the big pictures; integrates others' views.

COURAGE

_____ **Bravery:** valorous; does not shrink from fear; speaks up for what's right
_____ **Perseverance:** persistent; industrious; overcomes obstacles; finishes what is started
_____ **Authenticity, Integrity, & Honesty**: genuine; true to one's values; truthful
_____ **Zest:** enthusiastic; energetic; vital; feels alive and activated

HUMANITY

_____ **Love:** gives and accepts love; values close relations with others
_____ **Kindness:** generous; nurturing; caring; compassionate; altruistic
_____ **Social and/or Emotional Intelligence:** aware of the motives and feelings of oneself & others, know what makes other people tick

JUSTICE

_____ **Citizenship and/or Teamwork:** a team player; community-focused; socially responsible; loyal
_____ **Fairness:** acts upon principles of justice; does not allow feelings to bias decisions about others
_____ **Leadership**: organizes group activities; encourages and leads groups to get things done

TEMPERANCE

_____ **Forgiveness:** merciful; accepts others' shortcomings; gives people a second chance
_____ **Humility:** modest; lets accomplishments speak for themselves; focuses on others
_____ **Prudence:** careful; wisely cautious; thinks before speaking; does not take undue risks
_____ **Self-control:** self-controlled; disciplined; manages impulses & emotions

TRANSCENDENCE

_____ **Appreciation of Beauty & Excellence:** awe-filled; quickly moved to wonder; marvels at beauty & greatness
_____ **Gratitude:** thanks for the good; expresses thanks; feels blessed
_____ **Optimism & Hope:** optimistic; future-minded; has a positive outlook
_____ **Humor:** playful; enjoys joking and bringing smiles to others; lighthearted
_____ **Meaning, Purpose, & Spirituality:** meaning & purpose-driven, religious and/or spiritual

Appendix H: Relationship Appreciative Inquiry

This form is used in Chapter 13.

Your Name________________________ Their Name____________________________

Relationship appreciative inquiry is a process of recognizing the best in another person, reflecting on it and then saying or doing what you can do to improve your relationship and bring out the best in them.

	Question	Your Answer and Reflections on the Question
1	Why are they important to me?	
2	Why am I grateful to or for them?	
3	What do I appreciate about them?	
4	What strengths do I see in them?	

5	How can I best support them?	
6	How can I help them be their best, reach their goals, and be happy?	
7	What can I do to try to reduce or heal any wounds between us?	
8	What is the best gift that I can give to them?	
9	If they or I were to die tomorrow, what would I want to be sure to say to or do for them?	
10	Based upon my answers and reflections, what can I say or do to improve our relationship and their well-being?	

Appendix I: Acts of Kindness Planner

This planner is used in Chapter 15.

Instructions: Begin by reading through this list of kind acts and put a letter in the "Try" column to indicate those you would most like to try. Put an "A" for those you would most like to try, a "B" for those that aren't quite as high on your list, and a "C" for those you would like to consider again at some point. After you have tried any of them, put in a grade (A, B, C, D, etc.) to indicate how much of a positive impact doing the kind act had on you (in the "Self" column) and any others that the kind act was for (in the "Other" column).

A. Actions

		Try	Self	Other
1	Wash someone's dishes.			
2	Let a person at the coffee shop have the cream before you.			
3	Put stones with kindness quotes in random public places.			
4	Return shopping carts when you are walking into the store.			
5	Hold the elevator for someone or let people go in before you.			
6	Be kind to someone when they are being mean or rude to you.			
7	Save a parking spot for someone when you are leaving yours. (Flag them down)			
8	Grab the door for someone when they are coming in to a place that you are already in.			
9	Leave quarters in the quarter slot, enough for a load of laundry at the laundry mat.			
10	Give up your seat to anyone who needs it.			
11	Hold the door open for someone.			
12	Laugh wholeheartedly at someone's joke.			
13	Help someone put luggage into the overhead bin or grab it off the baggage claim line for them.			
14	Let someone get in line in front of you at the grocery store and tell them you have plenty of time.			
15	Tell someone a funny joke.			
16	Grab someone else's tray to dump at a fast-food restaurant.			
17	Offer to spot someone at the gym.			
18	Text a random number and tell them to have an awesome day!			
19	Post a string of motivational quotes on social media.			
20	Answer a question on Quora in your area of expertise to help someone out.			
21	Say happy birthday to someone you see when you get notified that it is their birthday on Facebook or other social media.			

22	Put a kind note in the pocket of jeans or a jacket at the store that tells them you hope they find what they are looking for.			
23	Let someone in when driving in traffic.			
24	Tell someone how funny you think they are.			
25	Be genuinely nice to someone who is cold calling you without feeling like you have to buy what they are selling.			
26	High five someone to help them celebrate something good for happening for them.			
27	Help someone fix a flat tire.			
28	Leave a newspaper or magazine for someone to read for free.			
29	Pick up weights or help unload weights for someone at the gym.			
30	Put a note one someone's car wishing them a good day.			

B. At Home

		Try	Self	Other
1	Unexpectedly, tell your spouse you love them.			
2	Practice identifying the strengths and positive qualities of friends and family members and them then tell about it.			
3	Call the person who was the biggest positive influence on your life and let them know how much they mean to you.			
4	Ask if you can grab anything for anyone when leaving the house or going outside the office.			
5	Do someone else's chore in your household.			
6	Put away dishes your roommates left out to dry while you are cleaning up.			
7	Do your roommate's laundry when you are doing yours.			
8	Let someone borrow your computer or printer.			
9	Clean the house so that your loved ones or roommates come home to a sparkling clean home.			

C. At Work

		Try	Self	Other
1	Help a friend find a job or a better job if they already have one.			
2	Praise a co-worker to your manager. Either in front of them or without them knowing.			
3	Praise your boss either verbally or through a thank you note			
4	Let someone know about a job opening that you saw.			
5	Make a pot of coffee when the coffee is low at the office.			
6	Bring donuts and coffee to your work one day.			
7	Clean out the microwave at work. That thing gets nasty and everyone will appreciate it			
8	Offer to cover a person's shift or work to give them time off.			
9	Bring extra food for lunch at work and give it away.			

10	Invite a co-worker or friend over for a home cooked meal.			
11	Make a meal for someone, breakfast in bed, or bring lunch to a co-worker.			
12	Bring a candy bar to a friend at work.			
13	Put a bowl of candy out at the office. Or, put out healthy snacks to promote wellness.			
14	Offer up one of your sick days to someone who really needs a day off or stay late for a co-worker who needs to get home.			
15	Create a connection with someone you know that can make for a good professional or personal contact.			

D. Caring/Empathy

		Try	**Self**	**Other**
1	Try to put yourself in the shoes of someone you are angry with, so you can better understand them.			
2	Be someone's accountability partner in helping them make a positive change.			
3	Offer someone a ride to an appointment or meeting where it takes forever to find parking.			
4	Offer to take someone's photo when they are trying to take one of themselves.			
5	Hold someone's hand when they are sharing their hurt or pain with you.			
6	Reach out to someone who you lost touch with and tell them how much the time with them meant to you.			
7	Give a bottle of water to a homeless person.			
8	Tell someone who is sick or has a broken limb that you hope they experience the quickest recovery ever.			
9	Pray for someone else and tell them you are praying for you.			
10	Go over and above to help someone who is lost. See if you can help them find their way.			
11	Ask someone you care about if you can give them a hug because they are so important to you.			
12	Turn your phone off when talking in person or put it away.			
13	Tell someone you believe in them.			
14	See the best in someone and tell them about it.			
15	Talk to a person you think is lonely to see how they are.			
16	Go play a game with someone at a retirement community.			
17	Use chalk to write a positive message or quote on the sidewalk of a street where a lot of people will see it.			
18	Ask someone who has suffered a loss how they are doing.			

19	Help an elderly or disabled person put their groceries in the car.			
20	Truly listen to someone without interrupting them.			
21	Make better eye contact when people are talking to you.			
22	Practice active constructive responding to share the excitement and celebrate with someone who has good news.			
23	Walk an elderly or disabled person across the crosswalk to make sure they get there safely.			
24	Pay someone a thoughtful compliment in front of others.			
25	Smile at every stranger you walk by on the street.			
26	Buy an umbrella to give to a homeless person when it is raining.			
27	Genuinely listen to someone with a different political viewpoint and thank them for helping you understand it.			
28	Write a motivational or encouraging message on a napkin and leave it at a restaurant or bar.			
29	Really listen to someone when they are upset without feeling like you have to tell them what to do.			
30	Don't interrupt someone when they are talking.			
31	Give the person next to you a word of encouragement at the gym to keep up with the healthy habit.			
32	Ask someone who you think experiences discrimination what it is like and if there is anything you can do to make it better.			
33	Stand up for someone who is being bullied or harassed.			
34	Ask someone you care about how you can help them achieve their goals or dreams.			

E. Children

		Try	Self	Other
1	Send school supplies to your local elementary school.			
2	Bring coloring books and crayons to pediatrics in the hospital.			
3	Tell a parent or child and tell them how you appreciate them.			
4	Leave some change at the playground for kids to find with a note telling them they are special.			
5	Help a mother carry her stroller over a curb or upstairs.			
6	Compliment a family on how nice they are in public.			
7	Let a friend who is a parent know your favorite quality about their child or how they parent their child.			
8	Sponsor a child in need.			
9	Go to the sports game of a friend's kid and cheer them on.			
10	Leave a dollar bill on the ground near where children are walking and watch how much joy they get from finding it.			
11	Read to children during story time at your local library			
12	Pay way more than kids charge at a lemonade stand.			
13	Babysit a friend's kid for free.			

F. Compliments/Encouragement

		Try	Self	Other
1	Compliment someone on their unique style or for being true to themselves.			
2	Tell someone you look up to them because they didn't give up.			
3	Text someone you care about and tell them you were thinking about them and hope they are well.			
4	Write a letter or email to someone you are grateful expressing your gratitude to them.			
5	Tell someone how much they mean to you			
6	Compliment someone on how well they have raised their kids.			
7	Dedicate a song on the radio to a friend, family member or loved one.			
8	Let a couple know how much you admire their relationship.			
9	Compliment someone's smile.			
10	Tell someone how nice their new haircut looks.			
11	Tell someone how good it is to see them.			
12	Text someone you just met up with or talked to about how you much enjoyed the conversation and the time they took to chat.			
13	Compliment someone's beard by saying how folically gifted they are.			
14	Say something super nice about someone who people are gossiping or saying bad things about.			
15	Tell someone how great they look that day or how what they are wearing looks nice.			
16	Write a letter or email to someone you love telling them how much you love and appreciate them.			
17	Tell someone how great they look in what they're wearing.			
18	Put positive comments on someone's blog.			
19	Tell someone you believe in them when they tell you they have something they want to achieve.			
20	Write a letter or email to someone you look up to telling them how much you admire them.			
21	Write an encouraging message, print out copies, and put them in public places where others will find them.			

G. Donations

		Try	Self	Other
1	Donate some of your gently worn shoes to "Soles4Souls."			

2	Donate old toys to Toys for Tots so less fortunate children around the world can have a great Christmas.			
3	Donate your computer to a student who may not be able to afford one.			
4	Become an organ donor.			
5	Ask people to donate to the homeless on social media and offer to pick up and deliver to a homeless shelter.			
6	Give your extra books to the library as a donation.			
7	Donate your old phone or charger to "Cell Phones for Soldiers"			
8	Donate to a cause when asked when checking out at a store.			
9	Create a Go Fund Me page for a cause you care about.			
10	Give your old bike to someone who doesn't have a car.			
11	Donate your hair to Locks of Love.			
12	Donate things you don't need any more to Goodwill.			
13	Participate in a fundraiser for a cause you care about.			
14	Donate clothing for someone who is homeless.			
15	Donate a pint of blood or plasma.			
16	Donate canned goods to a food pantry.			
17	Do a run or a walk for a cause you believe in.			

H. Family and Friends

		Try	Self	Other
1	Offer to house sit for a friend while they are on vacation.			
2	Text a simple "Good Morning" and tell them you hope they have a great day			
3	Offer to help a friend to unpack after they have moved or when they get home from a long trip.			
4	Bring in the neighbor's trash cans when you bring yours in.			
5	Help a friend move.			
6	Offer to be the designated driver one weekend.			
7	Give away your boxes to a friend that you know that is moving.			
8	Give away the last slice of pizza or cake.			
9	Pick someone up from the airport.			
10	Help with yard work.			
11	Help shop for deals for their next trip. Deals on travel, expenses, fun etc.			
12	Throw a block party and invite everyone.			
13	Buy a friend a week's worth of groceries.			
14	Bring a sick friend soup or something else they can enjoy.			
15	Buy a lottery ticket and put a note on it that you hope they win the big bucks.			
16	Encourage the person to go for their goals to get what they want.			

17	Wash the car of a friend or family member.			
18	Put a friend on your gym membership for a month to get them started with fitness.			
19	Throw a surprise party for someone you care about.			
20	Send a copy of a photo of a good memory to family or friend.			
21	Share discount coupons that you find.			
22	Wipe down the windshield of the car when you stop together at a gas station.			
23	Send an email of a funny joke.			
24	Tell someone what your favorite quality about them is.			
25	Throw out the trash on the way out of the house.			
26	Use social media to let someone know how big of an impact they have had on your life.			
27	Buy a book about someone or something you know they like.			
28	Send $20 Amazon gift card.			
29	Run an errand.			
30	Celebrate a victory or promotion by buying them lunch and asking them to tell you all about it.			
31	Send a song or song lyric that describes your relationship or what they mean to you.			
32	Call someone who is down or stressed and tell them you are there to help them get through it.			
33	Buy a bookmark for someone you know who loves to read.			
34	Send copies of an inspirational book.			
35	Create a digital album. Fill it with good memories or pictures you have taken of them.			
36	Create a thoughtful playlist for someone close to you.			
37	Make a custom-made shirt or hat.			
38	Give a sustainable water bottle that they can drink out of to help their health and save them money.			
39	Offer a ride to a friend who doesn't have a car or carpool with someone to help them save gas.			
40	Offer to go to shop for someone who is sick or stuck at home.			
41	Share your favorite recipe on social media.			
42	Write a poem to someone.			
43	Offer to babysit or kid sit, so the parent can get some time to themselves.			
44	Write a get-well card to someone who is sick			
45	Offer to read a book or magazine to a friend or loved one.			
46	Call and laugh about your favorite memory with them.			

47	Offer to do an errand.			
48	Befriend the new person at the gym, in town, at work or anywhere in your life.			
49	Text a motivational quote.			

I. Gifts

		Try	Self	Other
1	Share a cab with someone and pay the whole fare.			
2	Buy a bus ticket for someone.			
3	Put money in someone's meter so they don't get a ticket.			
4	Bake cookies or muffins and bring them to all the bank tellers at your preferred bank.			
5	Buy a fitness product for the person that always checks you in at the gym.			
6	Hand out bottles of hand sanitizer for people during flu season.			
7	Bring someone a souvenir or unique gift from somewhere you traveled to.			
8	Pass along a good book that you have just read to someone you think may appreciate it.			
9	Pay the road or bridge toll for the person driving behind you.			
10	Buy the movie ticket for the person in line behind you.			
11	Leave your bus pass on the bench when you are done with it for the day for someone else to find and use.			
12	Buy the food or drink of the person behind in the drive through.			
13	Buy an audio book for someone you know who commutes a lot.			
14	Buy a drink for a person that sits next to you at the bar.			
15	Give someone the gift of time.			
16	Leave extra money in the vending machine so someone can get a free snack.			
17	Buy a homeless person a meal.			
18	Offer a free weekend class that teaches kids what you know.			
19	Give a homeless person your jacket.			
20	Ask a waiter if they have recently received a bad tip and then make up for it by giving them extra money.			
21	Pay for the haircut of someone getting cut next to you.			
22	Bring extra coupons and give them out to people in line at the store you go to.			
23	Buy flowers for someone and put them where they will find them with a thoughtful note.			
24	Buy a sweet treat for someone else when you buy your own.			
25	Give someone else the cab that you flagged down.			

26	Return someone's book and/or pay off someone's past due library charges.			
27	Buy the groceries for someone behind you in the grocery line.			
28	Anonymously pay for someone's meal when dining out.			
29	Buy someone a flower and leave it where they will find it.			
30	Buy sunglasses for a homeless person if it is bright out.			

J. Kindness to/about Nature/Animals/The Environment

		Try	Self	Other
1	Give thanks to nature and the beauty it offers to us.			
2	Volunteer at the animal shelter and bring treats for the animals.			
3	Build a bird feeder and put food in it for birds.			
4	Feed some birds.			
5	Buy some toys for your friend's dog.			
6	Comb your friend's dog.			
7	Walk someone's dog for them.			
8	Put out a cup of water when you see a dog leashed up.			
9	Adopt an animal.			
10	Pet someone's dog and tell them how much you like their dog.			
11	Paint or clean off graffiti.			
12	Start to recycle more often.			
13	Pick up trash on your street or walking trail.			
14	Plant a tree or flowers in a place that could use them.			

K. Saying Thanks

		Try	Self	Other
1	Tip a musician who is playing on the street and wish him/her the best.			
2	Leave a large tip for a waiter or some other hospitality worker.			
3	Give someone working on your house, like a painter, electrician or plumber, a soda or cold glass of water.			
4	Tell your grocery checker you appreciate everything they do and hope they have a good day.			
5	Reach out and thank your favorite company or brand for the products or services they create.			
6	Thank a soldier for their service and offer to buy them lunch or coffee.			
7	Thank every veteran you meet for their service.			
8	Write a thank you letter to a soldier or veteran.			
9	Say thank you to anyone who helps you and mean it.			

10	Directly thank a police officer for the work they do.			
11	Send a note to the police station letting them know how much you appreciate them keeping you safe.			
12	Thank the cooks at a restaurant for cooking you such great food.			
13	Reach out to a former teacher letting them know how much you appreciate them.			
14	Wave to a firefighter or police officer to thank them for their service.			
15	Reach out to the pastor of your church and tell him or her how awesome their messages are.			
16	Thank the mail person for getting your mail to you on time.			
17	Tell the person who serves you coffee how much you appreciate the caffeine and how you wouldn't be the same without them!			
18	Leave an online review about how awesome a restaurant and/or server was.			
19	Thank your custodian for keeping your building clean.			
20	Tell an elderly person how much you appreciate their wisdom and life experience.			
21	Thank a parent for all they did to raise you.			
22	Call your grandparents and tell them how you loved what they did for you as a child.			
23	Send your mother or grandmother flowers.			

L. Kindness to One's Self

		Try	**Self**	**Other**
1	Get up a little earlier each morning and give gratitude for the things and people in life you are grateful for.			
2	Congratulate yourself for being a part of this challenge.			
3	Be kind to yourself by letting go of a mistake you made.			
4	Be kind to yourself by asking for help when you need it.			
5	Meditate for ten minutes as an expression of self-kindness.			
6	Write a forgiveness letter to yourself for something you did.			
7	Allow yourself to feel good about yourself for having read through this list.			
8	Write a forgiveness letter to someone who has harmed you and send it if you think it is appropriate.			
9	Meditate on what you can do to contribute to the happiness of another person in your life.			

Appendix J: Community Cause Inventory

This inventory is used in Chapter 16.

First, list the causes you care about that may affect the larger community and world. Second, rate the importance of each and your willingness and ability to do something to support each on a 0-10 scale where 0 = not at all and 10 = a great deal. Finally, rank the top three causes and write down something you can do to support each of the top three.

	Community Cause	How important is this cause to you?	How willing are you to do something for it?	How able are you to do something for it?
1				
2				
3				
4				
5				
6				
7				
8				
9				
10				
11				
12				

List and rank the three causes you would most like to support and write down something you can do to support each.

____

____

____

Appendix K: Guidelines for the PATH Process

The fourth part of the positive psychology challenge in this workbook involves creating a PATH poster as a roadmap to a better future. PATH is an acronym that stands for Planning Alternative Tomorrows with Hope and is a planning process developed by Jack Pearpoint, John O'Brien, and Marsha Forrest (Pearpoint et al., 2011). The PATH process involves creating a poster that shows your best possible life and what it may take for you to achieve it. After you create it, the poster can serve as a guide and reminder for achieving your goals.

The following diagram shows the shape and size of the poster and the steps that you will need to go through in creating it. The materials that you will need include colored writing utensils and two sheets of white poster board that you tape together on the short edges on the back as shown in the middle of the diagram. Medium point Sharpies work well for the writing because they are small enough to clearly and large enough to show up well on the poster. Common sizes of poster board are 22" x 28" and 24" x 36" and taping them together on the short end gives you a nice 44" x 56" or 48" x 72" surface for your poster.

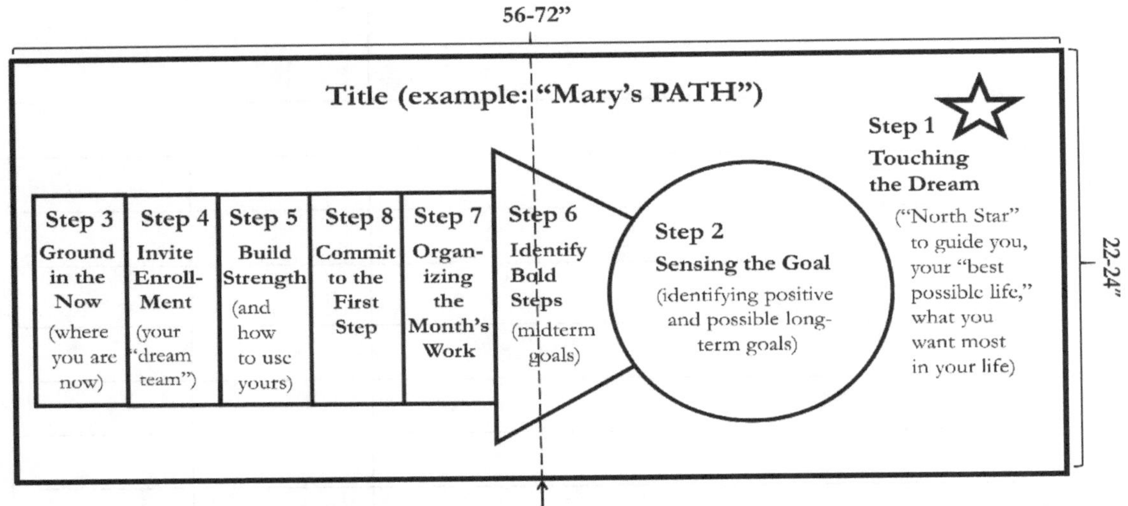

The dotted line shows where two sheets of poster board can be taped together on the back

Once of you've taped the sheets of poster board together, the next thing to do is to draw the lines that you see in the diagram above. These lines show where you will need to fill in for each of the eight steps. The diagram shows an arrow pointing from the left representing your life today to a circle on the right representing your best possible life in the future. The steps in the diagram do not go from left to right because these are the steps that you will take in completing the poster which begin with thinking about your dreams for the future.

Description of the Steps

Step 1. The first step is called **Touching the Dream** and involves envisioning a "North Star" that represents what you want most in life and filling in the part of the poster under the star in the upper right-hand corner of the poster. For this step, you need to write or draw things that show what your life would be like in the future if you could have anything you wanted. This is the place to dare to dream big even if you don't think it's realistic (e.g., "I'd like to be the next Einstein, Maya Angelou, Nelson Mandela, or Mother Teresa").

Step 2. The second step is called **Sensing the Goal** and involves identifying "positive and possible" goals for the future. While Step 1 involved what you'd like if there were no limits, Step 2 is where you identify realistic long-term goals and a specific time frame for achieving them (e.g., "Within the next 5 years, I'd like to get a graduate degree in physics and became a scientist or become a published poet and respected social activist"). You would write to describe or draw something to show these goals in the circle for Step 2.

Step 3. After having creating a realistic vision of a best possible future in Steps 1 and 2 on the right side of the poster, you go to the left side to focus on where you are now and how to achieve it. The third step is called **Ground in the Now** and involves identifying where you are in relation to your goals in Step 2. If one goal is to become a scientist or poet, you might describe your current experience with science or poetry in the box for Step 3.

Step 4. The fourth step is called **Invite Enrollment** and involves identifying and inviting people who can provide the encouragement and support that you may need to reach your long-term goals shown in Step 2. These people are called your "dream team" and you would put their names and what they you think they can do for you in the box for Step 4.

Step 5. The fifth step is called **Build Strength** and it involves listing your top strengths and how you can use them to reach your goals and listing the other strengths and skills you may need and how you can build and use them. You would put this in the box for Step 5.

Step 6. The final three steps involve making a practical plan to achieve your long-term goals by breaking them down into smaller parts. The sixth step is to **Identify Bold Steps** to achieve the long-term goals you set for yourself in Step 2. In the box for Step 6, you would list your goals for reaching a middle point in meeting your long-term goals.

Step 7. The seventh step is **Organizing the Month's Work** which involves being clear and specific about what you (and your dream team) will do in the next month to begin working to accomplish the mid-term goals you set in Step 6. Write this in the box for Step 7

Step 8. The eighth step is simply **Committing to the First Step** which means putting one thing in the box for Step 8 that you can do as soon as possible and then doing it!

Additional Resources:

1. Be sure to watch the following videos to better understand the PATH process:
    https://northstarfacilitators.com/the-path-process
    https://www.youtube.com/watch?v=_ecv_VN9KyI
    https://www.youtube.com/watch?v=LlKACFFEUdc
2. The following is an excellent brief workbook that walks you through the PATH process: Pearpoint, J., O'Brien, J., & Forest, M. (2011). *PATH: A workbook for planning positive possible futures.* Toronto, CA: Inclusion Press.
3. You can also email Tiffany Miner who is an experienced teacher of the PATH process with your questions at footprints93@gmail.com

Made in United States
Troutdale, OR
08/19/2024